LUCENT LIBRARY *of* HISTORICAL ERAS

MIRACLES, SAINTS, AND SUPERSTITION: THE
MEDIEVAL MIND

LUCENT LIBRARY *of* HISTORICAL ERAS

MIRACLES, SAINTS, AND SUPERSTITION: THE
MEDIEVAL MIND

LUCENT LIBRARY of HISTORICAL ERAS

MIRACLES, SAINTS, AND SUPERSTITION: THE
MEDIEVAL MIND

STEPHEN CURRIE

LUCENT BOOKS
A part of Gale, Cengage Learning

GALE
CENGAGE Learning

Detroit • New York • San Francisco • New Haven, Conn • Waterville, Maine • London

LIBRARY OF CONGRESS CATALOGING-IN-PUBLICATION DATA

Currie, Stephen.
  Miracles, saints, and superstition: The medieval mind / by Stephen Currie.
    p. cm.— (The Lucent library of historical eras. Middle Ages)
  Includes bibliographical references and index.
  ISBN 1-59018-861-6 (hard cover : alk. paper)   1. Church history—Middle Ages,
600–1500. 2. Religion. 3. Middle Ages. I. Title. II. Series.
BR162.3.C87 2006
940.1—dc22
                                                                          2006012436

Printed in the United States of America
4 5 6 7 12 11 10 09 08

Contents

Foreword

Looking back from the vantage point of the present, history can be viewed as a myriad of intertwining roads paved by human events. Some paths stand out—broad highways whose mileposts, even from a distance of centuries, are clear. The events that propelled the rise to power of Germany's Third Reich, its role in World War II, and its eventual demise, for example, are well defined and documented.

Other roads are less distinct, their route sometimes hidden from view. Modern legislatures may have developed from old tribal councils, for example, but the links between them are indistinct in places, open to discussion and interpretation.

The architecture of civilization—law, religion, art, science, and government—as well as the more everyday aspects of our culture—what we eat, what we wear—all developed along the historical roads and byways. In that progression can be traced every facet of modern life.

A broad look back along these roads reveals that many paths—though of vastly different character—seem to converge at a few critical junctions. These intersections are those great historical eras that echo over the long, steady course of human history, extending beyond the past and into the present.

These epic periods of time are the focus of Lucent's Library of Historical Eras. They shine through the mists of history like beacons, illuminated by a burst of creativity that propels events forward—so bright that we, from thousands of years away, can clearly see the chain of events leading to the present.

Each Lucent Library of Historical Eras consists of a set of books that highlight various aspects of these major eras. For example, the Elizabethan England library features volumes on Queen Elizabeth I and her court, Elizabethan theater, the great playwrights, and everyday life in Elizabethan London.

The mini-library approach allows for the division of each era into its most significant and most interesting parts and the exploration of those parts in depth. Also, social and cultural trends as well as illustrative documents and eyewitness accounts can be prominently featured in individual volumes.

Lucent's Library of Historical Eras presents a wealth of information to young readers. The lively narrative, fully documented primary and secondary source quotations, maps, photographs, sidebars, and annotated bibliographies serve as launching points for class discussion and further research.

In studying the great historical eras, students also develop a better understanding of our own times. What we learn from the past and how we apply it in the present may shape the future and may determine whether our era will be a guiding light to those traveling future roads.

◆ Introduction

THE MEDIEVAL PERIOD

The medieval period—very roughly, the era in western Europe between the fall of the Roman Empire around A.D. 400 and the beginning of the Renaissance in the late 1400s—has a powerful grip on the modern imagination. In the popular mind, the medieval era, also known as the Middle Ages, is closely associated with vivid images of knights and castles, swords and armor, violence and bravery. Modern movies and books from *The Da Vinci Code* and *The Once and Future King* to *Dragonheart* and *Monty Python and the Holy Grail* make use of medieval backdrops, story lines, and ideas. The drama and pageantry of the medieval era makes these years intriguing to people of the present day.

The medieval period is also attractive to many modern Americans because it seems to be a less complex and more appealing time. To modern eyes, life during the Middle Ages can seem less frenetic, less materialistic, and more oriented toward the rhythms of the natural world than it is today. Certainly, the people of the medieval period lived close to the earth in a way that most twenty-first-century Americans cannot emulate. In general, too, medieval castles, medieval fashions, and medieval bows and arrows strike many present-day Americans as both simpler and more romantic than the trappings of modern society, with its suburban subdivisions, shopping malls, and the ever-present threat of terrorism.

For all the allure of the medieval period, however, modern observers usually think of the Middle Ages as a stagnant era during which society changed very

Knights and nobles gather for an outdoor banquet during the Middle Ages.

karolus dei gratia francorum rex zc

little. For years, in fact, the period was widely known as the Dark Ages, an uncomplimentary reference to the supposed lack of science, learning, and other features of a civilized society during the time. The term "Dark Ages" has gone out of style now, but the medieval period is still often perceived as a backwater between two much greater eras: the ancient civilizations of Greece and Rome, which preceded the Middle Ages, and the Renaissance (literally, "rebirth") and Enlightenment, which followed them.

Changes and the Worldview

To some degree, this perception of the Middle Ages as static and unchanging is inaccurate. Castles gradually grew bigger and more formidable during the period, for instance, as weapons and battle strategies improved. Clothing

Farmers are shown going to town in this fourteenth-century painting. Medieval society did not question class differences.

styles and artistic preferences did not remain constant as time went on. The political structure of medieval society likewise changed considerably from the beginning of the period to its end. In particular, the Black Death of the 1300s caused massive economic and social change across Europe. And new ideas and customs constantly circulated from one region and people to another.

In other ways, though, it is fair to say that not much change took place during the Middle Ages. Medieval societies certainly did not enjoy the business and economic activity of Rome or Renaissance Italy. Nor, as a rule, were medieval philosophers and thinkers as influential as those of ancient Greece or the European Enlightenment of the 1700s. There was little emphasis on scientific thinking during the Middle Ages, and relatively little intellectual curiosity about how society worked—and why. The result was often an acceptance of the world as it was, an attitude that could and sometimes did lead to a lack of interest in creating or encouraging change.

The actions, or inactions, of societies are shaped in large part by their worldview—that is, by the way the people of the society perceive the world around them. The worldview of medieval society included ideas from many different sources, some of them contradictory. On the one hand, for instance, the people of the period were devoutly and enthusiastically Christian. On the other, the people of the Middle Ages drew many ideas and practices from the pagan faiths that preceded the arrival of Christianity. Similarly, medieval thinkers saw the world as at once good and evil, rational and absurd, pure and corrupt. These and other ideas about the world and the role of people in it defined the medieval worldview. They helped form medieval society, and they gave the medieval period its distinctive flavor.

Chapter One

CHRISTIANITY AND THE MEDIEVAL MIND

Christianity was the dominant religion in western Europe during the Middle Ages. As a result, the doctrines of the Christian faith were tightly connected to the medieval worldview. In dozens of ways, large and small, the ideas of the church formed the foundation of the medieval way of thinking. As one historian writes, during the Middle Ages Christianity "shaped everything and was shaped by everything."[1] To understand the medieval mind, then, means understanding the Christian religion of the period.

The Beginnings of Christianity

The Christian faith originated in the Middle East a few centuries before the medieval period began. Originally an outgrowth of Judaism, Christianity held that the Jewish prophet Jesus was the Messiah, or the Son of God. Christian teachings described how Jesus incurred the wrath of powerful leaders in the Middle East and how he was eventually sentenced to death. According to Christian theology, Jesus chose not to use his powers to save himself; instead, he atoned for the sins of all humanity by allowing himself to be crucified, or killed by being nailed to a cross.

To Christians, however, Jesus's death was not the end of the story. Three days after his crucifixion, they believe, Jesus triumphed over the grave by coming back to life. In this view, Jesus's sacrifice opened the door to eternal life for all Christians and pointed the way toward a new world of justice, plenty, and peace. As the biblical book of John puts it, "God sent his son into the world not to condemn the world, but so that through him the world might be saved" (John 3:17). The promise of salvation of souls, as a result, was central to Christian doctrine.

A small, persecuted, and secretive sect in its early existence, Christianity nonetheless spread slowly through the lands that bordered the Mediterranean Sea. It picked up converts from Judaism, the religion from which it had sprung. It also attracted new believers from among the other faiths of the Roman Empire. The bulk of these new converts came from pagan religions, faiths whose members worshipped multiple gods. In paganism, each god or goddess usually took on a specific area of responsibility; one might be in charge of love, another of war, a third of the hunt. In Christianity, however, as in Judaism, there was just one God.

A Growing Faith

Through the 100s and the 200s, Christianity spread around the Mediterranean region and occasionally beyond. Its growth troubled Roman authorities, who saw it as a potential threat to the power of the established pagan faiths. Some officials tried to suppress the new religion by imprisoning Christians or even executing them. Still, the hold of Christianity on the Roman population did not diminish. By the year 300, despite the dangers of professing the Christian faith, thousands of people in the Roman Empire had become adherents of the new religion.

As Christianity grew in numbers, it also began to grow in power. In 313 the

A ninth-century painting depicts Jesus's crucifixion. Christianity originated in the Middle East several centuries before the Middle Ages.

A beardless Jesus presents a scroll to doctors in this fourth-century casket relief. By the 400s, Christianity was a widely accepted religion.

Roman emperor Constantine removed the penalties against the practice of Christianity. More than that, Constantine favored Christianity in his policies and encouraged the people of the empire to join the faith. In 395 a later emperor, Theodosius, went further and declared Christianity the official state religion. His announcement marked the end of a remarkable transformation. Despised only a century before, Christians had become the most powerful people in Rome.

The Roman Empire did not last long after Theodosius's proclamation. Just fifteen years after he issued his edict, in fact, the city of Rome was invaded by soldiers from northern Europe. Sensing Rome's vulnerability, other groups quickly attacked lands and peoples that had long been a part of the vast Roman Empire. The Franks conquered large sections of what is now France. The Angles and the Saxons ended Roman domination in Britain. Other groups seized Spain and North Africa. By the year 500, the Roman Empire was no more.

But though Rome was no longer powerful, the faith that Theodosius and Constantine had championed was flourishing. That was true even though the church eventually fractured into two separate organizations—one, the Western or Catholic Church, based in Rome; the other, the Eastern or Orthodox Church, based in Constantinople. Missionaries from the Catholic Church moved north and west, converting pagans who lived in the areas that are now Austria, Germany, and Switzerland. Later they traveled to England and made it a predominantly Christian country. France, Ireland, Italy, and the Netherlands—each was brought into the Christian fold. By 1000 the Catholic Church's spread across western Europe was more or less complete.

God and Satan, Good and Evil

The basic tenets of Christianity are contained in the books of the Bible, which consists of two parts. The Hebrew Bible, often called the Old Testament by Christians today, includes many of the most sacred and familiar stories of Judaism, such as Noah and the Flood, Moses and the Ten Commandments, and Adam and Eve and the Garden of Eden. Early

Muslims and Jews

Not all medieval Europeans were Christians. Muslims and Jews made up small but significant parts of the population as well. Muslims, indeed, ruled Spain and Portugal during much of the Middle Ages. At times, Christians tolerated the presence of Islam in the region, in part because Muslims of the period were often wealthy and well armed, and accepted Islam as what one historian calls "a separate [and] legitimate if somewhat inferior religion, not as a dreaded heresy." At other times, however, Christians fought the Muslims in Europe and elsewhere with hatred and violence.

Unlike European Muslims, European Jews held no political power. They were scattered across the region, especially prevalent in Spain and parts of Germany, but nowhere did they make up a majority. Some Jews were farmers, others merchants. While Jews in business often amassed great wealth and occupied positions of privilege, there was always an undercurrent of hostility directed toward them by Christian officials and sometimes by temporal authorities as well. Especially during the later medieval period, Jews were also blamed for disasters and subjected to restrictive laws. By 1500, because of prejudice and threats, especially in areas west of Germany, Jews were increasingly resettling in eastern Europe.

Quoted in Norman F. Cantor, ed., *The Encyclopedia of the Middle Ages.* New York: Viking, 1999, p. 246.

Christians accepted the books of the Hebrew Bible as both holy and literally true. At the same time, the new religion also incorporated new texts. These included writings about Jesus's life, death, and resurrection, along with reports about the acts of Jesus's early followers and prophecies of what was to come. These writings are known collectively as the books of the New Testament.

As outlined in part in the Bible and in part by later theologians, Christian doctrine sees the world as a fundamental struggle between two great forces: the force of good, as represented by God, and the force of evil, as represented by Satan, or the devil. Just as medieval Christians believed wholeheartedly in a literal God, so too did they accept the existence of a literal devil. In Christian theology, Satan tempted humans to turn away from God and toward sin and evil. An army of demons, loyal assistants who did his bidding, helped him carry out this task.

Despite Satan's apparent powers, Christians believed that he was not the equal of God. At some point in the future, Christian doctrine explained, God would destroy the devil and triumph over evil. Jesus's resurrection was taken as a portent of that coming event. In the meantime, however, evil was believed to be a real presence in the world, and Satan was considered a genuine being. "He could enter the human body and force it into evil acts," writes author Charles Panati, summarizing the powers of the devil as medieval Christians saw him. "He could jump from one body into another."[2] Christians had to be constantly on guard against him and his minions.

How people responded to God and Satan—to good and evil—was of great importance in Christian theology. Christians of the medieval era viewed life as a test. Those who chose God while on earth could expect rewards in the afterlife. Those who rejected God and turned instead toward Satan, in contrast, could expect punishment and torture. To the people of the Middle Ages, the existence of a next world was a given. The only question was into which part of that next world a particular soul would go.

Heaven, Hell, and in Between

The worst possible destination was hell, the domain of Satan and his army of demons. Those whose sins on earth were great, whose hearts were full of anger and hatred, or who had not followed the teachings of the church would spend the rest of eternity in hell, or so medieval Christians believed. Hell, by all accounts, was a ghastly place. "In Hell," writes historian Barbara Tuchman, summing up the popular images of the time, "the damned hung by their tongues from trees of fire, the impenitent [those who were not sorry for their sins] burned in furnaces, unbelievers smothered in foul-smelling smoke."[3]

Other souls were sent to purgatory, a sort of holding tank for those who had sinned but were not beyond redemp-

A thirteenth-century mosaic represents hell, believed by medieval Christians to be a place where people were sent if they did not obey God.

tion. Once in purgatory, these souls were subject to punishments to remove the last vestiges of sin. Another possible destination for souls who did not qualify for hell was limbo, populated by babies who had died before baptism and by non-Christians who were nonetheless decent human beings. The souls in hell were believed to have no chance of redemption, but medieval Christians generally accepted that those in purgatory and limbo would eventually be saved.

The most desired destination of all, of course, was heaven. In contrast to hell, heaven was a place of peace and beauty, of leisure and ease: a place where God reigned in glory and showed his favor to his people. In heaven, according to Revelation 22:5, "it will never be night again, and they [the souls brought there after death] will not need lamplight or sunlight, because the Lord God will be shining on them." Later writers added images of their own. The Italian poet Dante

Alighieri, for instance, used metaphors of light, sound, and nature to describe the paradise that awaited the good. In comparison to the glorious music of heaven, Dante wrote, "the sweetest melody heard upon earth . . . would be like a cloud split by thunder."[4]

Unfortunately, as medieval Christians saw it, only a very small proportion of souls would actually be admitted into heaven. Only the holiest of all people, perhaps as few as one in ten thousand, would qualify. It might not even be enough to attend church regularly, to show genuine repentance for sins, and to follow Jesus's injunctions to "love the Lord your God with all your heart" (Matt. 22:37) and to "love your neighbor as yourself" (Matt. 22:39). No one truly knew God's mind and heart. Still, the prospect of an eternity in hell encouraged many medieval Europeans to live as godly a life as they could manage.

Regardless of what they believed to be their ultimate destination, Christians of the Middle Ages perceived life as temporary and difficult. In the Christian view, life was not about joys and pleasures; these awaited the good in the next world. Instead, life was a testing ground whose ultimate purpose was the separation of the people of God from the people of Satan. As the Italian writer Petrarch explained, life was "a hard and

Money and the Church

The role of money in the church was a major issue through much of the Middle Ages. Though many monks in particular took vows of poverty when they entered religious life, and though the Bible portrayed Jesus and his disciples as poor and humble men, money was nevertheless influential in church affairs. Ambitious priests bribed officials to make them bishops. Wealthy nobles paid to have their daughters admitted to convents and their sons admitted to the priesthood, whether they were qualified or not. Toward the end of the Middle Ages especially, priests and other religious leaders openly sold indulgences— that is, they offered pardon from sin in exchange for money.

All of this money served to make the church—and many of its clergymen, particularly popes—quite rich. As the Italian writer Petrarch pointed out in disgust during the 1300s, the popes of his time were "loaded with gold and clad in purple." Resentment over the wealth of the popes, the sale of indulgences, and the overall role of money in church business eventually helped rip the church in two during the Protestant Reformation of the early 1500s, not long after the end of the medieval era.

Quoted in Barbara Tuchman, *A Distant Mirror: The Calamitous 14th Century.* New York: Knopf, 1978, p. 27.

weary journey toward the eternal home for which we look; or, if we neglect our salvation, an equally pleasureless way to eternal death."[5] Heaven or hell, good or evil: as the people of medieval Christendom saw it, humans made a choice—and took the consequences.

A Pyramid of Authority

By the Middle Ages, the Christian Church was set up as a hierarchy; that is, it was structured like a pyramid. The foundation of the pyramid was made up of monks, nuns, and priests. All had taken religious vows that required them to remain celibate and to follow the rules of the church. Monks lived together in monasteries and engaged in prayer, outreach to nearby communities, and often other work as well. Nuns, who were housed in convents, were roughly the female equivalent of monks. Life in a convent or monastery was strict, silent, and spartan; one historian writes, "The religious life was not, nor was it intended to be, an easy one."[6] But many who chose it found satisfaction in its structures, rhythms, and tasks.

While monks and nuns tended to look inward, priests looked outward. Most priests lived and worked at small churches in villages or on large estates owned by noblemen. Like the monks, all of these priests were male; many were drawn from the peasantry. The priests were assigned to run the churches and to take care of the people of their parish or community. "It was the humble vil-

lage cleric," writes one historian, "who carried the weight of medieval religiosity and integrated it into the daily life of ordinary people."[7] Together, monks, nuns, and priests carried out much of the work of the church throughout medieval Europe.

These lower religious orders, in turn, answered to bishops and archbishops, priest-administrators who oversaw dozens of different churches and sometimes convents and monasteries as well. Bishops had the power—and the responsibility—to discipline those in religious life who did not conduct themselves according to expectation. "We visited at Ste-Catherine, where there are thirty monks," wrote Archbishop Odo of Rouen, France, in the 1200s. "Caleboche and another monk, who are now in prison, sing dissolute [immoral] songs; we ordered that they be corrected by cutting off their food and subjecting them to flagellation [beatings]."[8]

The bishops, however, were not the final authority. They were outranked by the pope, the spiritual leader of Western Christianity. The pope was responsible for the workings of the entire church. Chosen by veteran bishops known as cardinals, the pope was elected for life. The power of the pope varied somewhat from decade to decade and from century to century, but for the most part—especially in the later Middle Ages—the pope's word reigned supreme within the church. One observer characterized the pope as "no longer man,

A monk provides spiritual guidance as he preaches to his attentive congregation.

not yet wholly God,"[9] and the description was apt.

The Spiritual and the Worldly

The Church of Rome existed primarily as a spiritual institution. It held worship services, offered pardon for sins, and pointed the way to heaven. Indeed, the church focused most of its energy on matters of the spirit. Theologians debated difficult religious questions regarding the nature of God, the path to forgiveness, the meaning of stories in the Bible, and much more. Monks and nuns did their best to ease the sufferings of the sick and the poor. Priests reminded their flocks of the need to lead a godly life. And religious leaders of all kinds prayed frequently. "God is to be praised at every hour of the day,"[10] wrote thirteenth-century author Jacob de Voragine.

Church officials, however, did not limit their focus to issues of religious doctrine and faith. Ever since Theodosius declared Christianity the official religion of the Roman Empire, the Christian faith had been tightly connected to temporal, or worldly, matters as well. When the Roman Empire collapsed, notes one historian, "the pope in effect replaced the emperor as chief official in Rome, responsible for importing grain . . . as well as for negotiating with the German invaders."[11] As time went on, the temporal powers of the church remained. From popes and bishops to monks and priests, the church had not just spiritual authority but also political power—and was extremely eager to exercise it.

Thus, medieval taxes typically supported not only kings and castles but priests and cathedrals as well. In the same way, marriage was at once a religious rite and a legal matter. As a general principle, the rules of the established church were often identical to the laws of the state. Not only were crimes such as murder or robbery forbidden by both the church and by the various governments of Europe, but challenges to the institution of Christianity were frequently prosecuted by temporal authorities as crimes. For example, medieval Europeans accused of heresy—that is, opposing or violating church doctrine —were subject to civil trial and punishment by governments and the church.

Church and State

Not every temporal ruler during the Middle Ages was under the thumb of the pope. On the contrary, some kings and other nobles rose to a level of authority that rivaled the pope's. And on a few occasions, extremely powerful leaders did manage to overcome the political authority of the church. During the early 1000s, for instance, the papacy, or office of the pope, was subordinate to the rulers of Germany. The same was true in France, first under the emperor Charlemagne during the 800s, and then again under a series of different rulers during the 1300s.

Yet even when popes had to submit to the will of a more powerful civil ruler, the ideas of Christianity still pervaded society. No ruler dared reject the authority of the church out of hand; none called the basic tenets of Christianity into question; none attempted to abolish the papacy altogether. Throughout the medieval period, a crime against the church remained a crime against the state, and even strong rulers made a show of giving tax revenues to Christian authorities to build cathedrals and help the poor. It was one thing to challenge the rule of a specific pope; it was quite another for a government or leader to reject the church itself.

To modern Americans accustomed to sharp divisions between church and state, this blurring of roles may seem peculiar. In medieval Europe, however, it was unremarkable. "To be part of [medieval] society," sums up historian

Heresy

The medieval church devoted much attention to the problem of heresy. Many alternative doctrines appeared among Christians during the Middle Ages. The Donatists, for example, believed that sacraments given by an incompetent or unworthy priest were not valid, a view in direct opposition to that of the established church. Another group, the Albigensians, argued that there were in effect two gods—one god of light and good, and one of darkness and evil. This was similar, of course, to the Christian conception of God and Satan. The established church, however, saw Satan as fundamentally less powerful than God, while the Albigensians held that good and evil were of approximately equal strength.

To the church, these and similar doctrines were grave errors and therefore heresies. Church officials moved quickly to stamp them out, by persuasion if possible, but by force if necessary. "There must be no arguing with heretics," ran a maxim of the 1200s. "If [a heretic] refuses to believe, he must be condemned." Heretics who persisted in their beliefs, in fact, were sometimes killed. Nonetheless, Europeans dissatisfied with the teachings of the Catholic Church continued to seek out new ways of understanding and interpreting standard Christian doctrines—to the chagrin and outrage of the church.

Quoted in Friedrich Heer, *The Medieval World.* New York: New American Library, 1961, p. 215.

Jeffrey Singman, "was to be part of the church."[12] Since Christians of the time saw the entire world as connected to their faith, Christian ideas on virtually everything came to affect the medieval worldview. From conceptions of time to images of the afterlife, from the role humans played on earth to ideas of healing, Christian beliefs shaped the way medieval Europeans thought about their lives—and the way they thought about the world around them.

Chapter Two

TIME
AND SPACE

The way a culture views time and space can offer important insight into that culture's worldview. The level of detail on a society's maps, for example, indicates in part the scientific progress of the society, but it can also reveal how the people of that culture feel about the world around them. Similarly, the methods used by a certain culture to measure and calculate time reflect some of that culture's values. Medieval Europe is no exception. The way the people of this culture thought about time and space both mirrored and shaped the worldview of the period.

Clock Time

To a modern observer, medieval Europe is perhaps especially notable for its apparent lack of interest in clock time, the division of the day into hours, minutes, and seconds. Europeans of the Middle Ages seldom spoke of specific times. As one modern commentator observes, "There was no such thing as having a 3:15 appointment"[13] during the Middle Ages. Indeed, writers of the period rarely used words any more specific than "afternoon" and "evening." Dawn, dusk, and noon—when the sun rose, set, and stood directly overhead—were meaningful times, noted by writers; the hours and minutes between these moments, generally speaking, were not.

For that matter, during the medieval period the length of an hour was not necessarily fixed at sixty minutes. Instead, one hour—when the concept was used at all—most often represented one-twelfth of the period between sunrise and nightfall. The length of an hour, as a result, varied according to season. During the summer, an hour was much longer than a standard hour today. In the dead of winter, on the

A woman holds an hourglass, a medieval instrument that measured time by the amount of sand that fell from one end to the other.

other hand, it was a good deal shorter. The vagueness of the measurement indicates the loose conception of clock time common to the people of the medieval period.

There was a practical reason for the medieval lack of precision: the scarcity of working clocks. Through most of the medieval period, people typically measured time by using sundials, sand timers, and other inexact devices. These materials made it difficult enough to tell time to the hour, and essentially impossible to divide it any further than that. Even in the late Middle Ages, when me-

chanical clocks became more common, evidence indicates that most did not keep time very accurately. The first mechanical clocks had just one hand, which marked the hour. The minute hand did not appear until near the close of the medieval period.

But the reason for the imprecision went well beyond practicalities. The reality of life during the Middle Ages made it unnecessary to keep careful track of minutes—or even of hours. Most people of the era made their living through farming, an occupation that had little need for precise measurements of time. Farmers typically rose with the sun and worked throughout the day. No one came in from the fields at 5:00 P.M., and no one would have done so regularly even if there had been a means of measuring the time accurately. Agricultural society did not ignore the passage of time, but this passage was marked by the rhythms of nature rather than by the artificial divisions of a clock.

Calendar Time

Medieval Europeans paid closer attention to calendar time—the passage of days, weeks, months, and years. The units of time used during the medieval period were largely the same as those used today. Medieval weeks had seven days, for example, and medieval years were made up of twelve months. The names of the days and the months were often mentioned in legal documents and in personal accounts. "The Great Khan [ruler of China]," wrote the famous traveler Marco Polo in the 1200s, "usually resides during three months of the year, namely December, January, and February, in the great city of Kanbalu."[14]

Though medieval measurements of clock time tended toward the imprecise, the people of the Middle Ages were usually somewhat more specific where calendar time was concerned. Writers of the time often, though not always, noted the year in which important events had taken place. A few recorded the month and number of the day as well. "On the following day, 9th April," read one contemporary account of the decision to make Urban VI the new pope in 1378, "the election was made known to the officials and governors of the city of Rome."[15]

Even so, the concept of calendar time during the medieval period was not quite the same as the concept of calendar time today. The medieval year did not necessarily begin on January 1, for example. Depending on the time and the place, it began instead on Easter Sunday, on Christmas Day, or on March 25. There was little or no uniformity across the entire continent during the period.

Dates and Years

The real issue was not so much the specifics of the medieval calendar as the way people of the era thought about calendars. Many medieval Europeans ignored standard ways of expressing large units of time. As a result, rather than noting years by writing "1372" or "954," for instance, medieval writers often measured years by counting from an important recent event, such as the death of a pope or a destructive local fire. "The king ordered me by letter to be with him at York . . . in the sixteenth year of his reign,"[16] wrote an English noblewoman in 1326.

Nor did most chroniclers refer to specific dates in their writing. When they wanted to fix an event in time, they generally described it in terms of the nearest Christian holy day or other celebration of the church year. It was assumed that the audience knew when each day took place. "King Richard . . . set out with a great army," wrote medieval chronicler Adam of Usk, "landing on the feast of St. Mary Magdalene,"[17] or July 22. Another chronicler, Jean Froissart, used the phrase "the Monday next after the feast of Whitsuntide"[18] where a modern writer would simply have written "June 2."

This way of giving dates reflected the influence of the Christian Church in everyday life during the medieval period. Virtually every published calendar of the time noted major Christian feast days and other religious occasions—and many minor occasions as well. To medieval Europeans, in fact, determin-

Pictured is a page from a fifteenth-century calendar. The top represents June, while the bottom shows peasants harvesting a field at that time of the year.

ing the progression of these days was the main reason to keep or consult a calendar. In ordinary life, it scarcely mattered whether a given day was, for example, March 31 or April 1, but it was essential to know when the solemn occasion of Good Friday or the joyous festival of Easter Sunday took place.

Just as the agricultural basis of medieval society reduced the need for clock time, so too did it make calendar time relatively unimportant. The days and

The Christian Calendar

The Christian year included quite a variety of holidays, some major and celebrated throughout Europe, others minor. They were of two kinds: movable and fixed. A fixed holiday appears each year on the same date. Christmas, for example, is a fixed holiday, always appearing on December 25. The Feast of the Epiphany, which commemorates the arrival of the wise men to visit the baby Jesus, is similarly observed on January 6 each year.

Other Christian feast days are—and were—movable. That is, they are not necessarily held on the same date from one year to the next. Easter Sunday, for instance, is tied to the spring equinox and the phases of the moon. Thus, it can occur anywhere between late March and mid-April. Ash Wednesday, which marks the beginning of the Lenten season, is another movable holiday. So is Pentecost, a feast held in late spring or early summer that celebrates the descent of the Holy Spirit—one manifestation of God—among Jesus's disciples. The multiplicity of movable holidays in the Christian calendar can make it difficult for modern historians to translate medieval dates into standard months and days.

months of the year followed a rhythm that had little to do with specific dates. Spring planting, for example, did not occur every year on the same date; instead, it took place whenever the ground was ready for seeds, a determination that varied from year to year. Similarly, a farmer might hope to have his crops harvested by October 15, but the weather could—and often did—have other ideas. In general, there was little point in linking most farm responsibilities to individual dates.

The Cycle of Time

The hour, the day, and even the year, then, mattered little to the people of the Middle Ages. Instead, the basic unit of time in the medieval era was the season. The agricultural calendar, of course, was centered on the seasons of spring, summer, fall, and winter. The church calendar followed a progression of seasons as well, each with its own characteristics. The Christmas season, for instance, was a time of celebration that lasted for twelve days after the winter solstice; the season of Lent, in contrast, was a period of fasting and introspection in winter and the early part of spring.

The emphasis on seasons made sense for a rural, deeply Christian society like medieval Europe. It also provides a window into the medieval way of thinking. What the people of the Middle Ages valued was the cyclical sweep of time. To an extent, of course, this focus on the rotation of events remains true today:

The sequence of days repeats itself every week, as does the order of months within a year. Nonetheless, to medieval eyes the focus on the constant repetition of seasons was all encompassing.

Yet medieval Europeans in general did not see themselves as a part of a sweep of history. They did not typically believe that they had the power to change the world around them for the better, except in small ways. Neither did they accept that changes in the world around them could push them into new ways of thinking and acting. They saw the world instead as a fundamentally stable and static place in which nothing much changed. "There was little sense of progress," notes historian Jeffrey Burton Russell. "For the most part, medieval men ignored the idea that human events were leading anywhere."[19]

To Europeans of the Middle Ages, then, time was not primarily about forward movement. Neither was it fundamentally a tool for determining the exact length of an hour or a day. Instead, the medieval understanding of time reflected society's focus on religion and agriculture. It also emphasized the medieval notion that the world was at heart a motionless and unchanging place. Winter was different from fall, to be sure, and Lent was scarcely the same as Christmas—but to medieval thinkers, the essential truth was that these seasons and holidays had come around again and again for hundreds of years, and would presumably continue to do so as long as the world endured.

Lords and ladies participate in a Christmas dance. During the Middle Ages, the Christmas season lasted for twelve days after the winter solstice.

Travel

Like medieval notions of time, medieval ideas of geography also impacted and reflected the overall worldview during the Middle Ages. There were Europeans during these years who traveled widely and visited distant places. The Vikings of Scandinavia sailed to Iceland, Greenland, and the coast of North America beginning in the 800s. Italian merchant Marco Polo spent many years in China and central Asia during the 1200s. And Christian knights who took part in the Crusades,

attacks on the Muslim-held regions of the Middle East, also visited places that were far from western Europe.

Other medieval Europeans also traveled, if less often or less far. Kings toured their kingdoms, and high-ranking church officials visited churches and cathedrals throughout a region or an entire country. Peasants and nobles occasionally ventured on pilgrimages, religious journeys to holy places such as Rome, and soldiers often traveled to other countries to fight. From time to time, too, people

Eleventh Century Medieval Europe

Norway

Scotland

Sweden

Denmark

Lithuanians

Ireland

Anglo-Saxon Kingdom

Prussians

Russia

Wales

Poland

Holy Roman Empire

France

Hungary

Burgundy

Navarre

Croatia

Petchenegs

Leon

Servia

Barcelona

Corsica

Bulgaria

Cordova

Sardinia

Byzantine Empire

Lombardy

Sicily

Calabria

Dominion of the Fatimites

moved from one place in Europe to another, usually for economic gain or to escape violence. "Foreigners from Holland . . . began to settle on the southern bank of the Elbe"[20] in eastern Germany, a medieval priest noted in a chronicle covering the region.

Still, the majority of medieval Europeans seldom, if ever, ventured far from their birthplaces. Much of the reason involved issues of transportation. Since no vehicles of the time had engines, travel of any distance required considerable time. Sailing ships were at the mercy of the winds and the waves, and most medieval sailors did not dare take their vessels much beyond the sight of the coast. Land travelers found few good roads, only narrow winding paths that led from one community to the next. Worse yet, robbers and kidnappers often lurked along the best-traveled routes. Given the hazards and uncertainties of travel, most medieval Europeans simply stayed home.

Localism

Because so few medieval Europeans traveled, the people of the continent had little knowledge of the world beyond Europe's borders—and often little knowledge of the world even a few dozen miles from their homes. This was particularly true in the first half of the Middle Ages. "The early medieval period was a time of localism," writes one historian, "when consciousness of and interest in distant lands evaporated."[21] This general attitude prevailed, if less powerfully, until the beginning of the Renaissance.

The result was a sharply restricted worldview. People of the Middle Ages tended to define themselves as belonging to a small geographic area rather than to a region, a country, or the continent of Europe. Sometimes this area of allegiance was a village or a town. For the serfs, members of a class of peasants who worked on estates belonging to more powerful nobles, the basic geographical unit was usually smaller still —it was the estate itself. By law, these serfs had to remain on the land unless their lord gave them permission to leave. Quite literally, they belonged to the estate. Knowing little of the land beyond its boundaries, and recognizing that they would probably never live anywhere else, the serfs of the era focused their attention on the small piece of land they called home.

Whether medieval Europeans identified with their town, their estate, or even with a region of a country, the localism of the time resulted in a fragmented perspective. The residents of one estate did not necessarily feel connected to the people of another estate just a few miles removed. The same was true of residents of larger towns and cities. Rich and powerful nobles may have thought of themselves as French, English, or Spanish, but many ordinary Europeans of the time lacked even a regional identity, let alone a national one. Medieval Europe, writes historian Friedrich Heer, "was a community made up of some ten thousand smaller houses and a few hundred greater houses . . . all seeking to assert themselves, and forming alliances against each other."[22]

This insular way of thinking helped create a society that was relatively closed. Certainly, the disjointed identities of medieval Europe discouraged cooperation and unity. Especially in early medieval Europe, this lack of cooperation hindered trade among countries and towns and often sparked warfare between neighboring peoples. Throughout the period, moreover, it led to hostility against people who looked, acted, or thought differently. At various times, Jews, Muslims, and heretics suffered scorn, abuse, and worse. Jews, whom Christians already blamed for the crucifixion of Christ, were in particular

Medieval Maps

Maps were used during the Middle Ages, but medieval maps were very different from the maps that are used today. Most gave little indication of distances and only vaguely represented the actual sizes and shapes of the areas they showed. To travel from one place to another, people of the time relied largely on oral directions and signposts rather than on any information found on a map. The few analogues to modern road maps during medieval times simply showed landmarks along a particular route in the order in which they would be encountered.

Other medieval maps were created to serve as schematics, or organizers. World maps from the early Middle Ages, for example, showed the world as a circle with the city of Jerusalem—the holiest place in Christian tradition—at the center. East was typically at the top of the map, so the upper half of the circle showed Asia—the land to the east of Jerusalem. The bottom half of the circle was divided between Europe and Africa. The overall effect was that of a T inscribed inside an O, and today these maps are often known as T-O maps. Since T-O maps lacked detail and accuracy, they were useless in navigation or in understanding the world that lay beyond Europe's borders. But they did reflect the value medieval Europeans placed on Jerusalem and their passion for organizing the world around them.

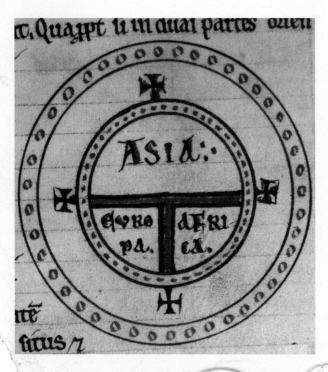

A T-O map displays Jerusalem at the center, with Asia, Europe, and Africa surrounding it.

A fourteenth-century painting depicts two fighting sea monsters. Medieval Europeans believed such creatures existed in faraway waters.

suspected of causing the Black Death of the 1300s by poisoning water supplies. Many Jews were tortured and put to death as a result.

The Outside World

If the Europeans of the time knew little about their own continent, they had only a very dim notion of what lay be- yond its borders. Africa, they knew, lay across the Mediterranean Sea, but no one had any idea just how large Africa actually was, or what lay beyond the narrow coastal strip known to Euro- peans. Knights on the Crusades visited the Middle East, and European mer- chants carried out occasional trade with merchants in this area; still, their knowledge of the region typically was

Time and Art

Medieval art often reflects the medieval sense of time, especially where historical art is concerned. As historian Barbara Tuchman writes, "Medieval artists made no distinction between past and present." It was not that medieval artists made use only of images from the world around them; on the contrary, many medieval painters looked to history for their subjects. They did not place these pictures in a historical context, however. Instead of including the details of a given historical period in their work, artists typically painted everything as if it were happening in their own era. Thus, a painting showing a battle scene from history, for example, would include standard military equipment dating from the time the picture was created, not from the time of the original battle. In this way, the painting—while nominally of a single event—actually stands for all battles through all time.

Quoted in Barbara Tuchman, *A Distant Mirror: The Calamitous 14th Century.* New York: Knopf, 1978, p. 108.

limited to a few parts of Turkey and Lebanon. As for the rest of Asia, Europeans knew it existed, but how far east it extended or what sorts of people lived there were open questions.

Nor did most Europeans of the Middle Ages care to visit these distant lands. The robbers, heretics, and other unfamiliar peoples who populated the rest of Europe seemed alarming enough. The stories told about the peoples and landscapes of Africa and Asia, on the other hand, were truly terrifying. If a sailor ventured far enough south along the African coast, so one rumor went, the sea around him would begin to bubble and boil. Another tale told of the giants Gog and Magog, who lived somewhere beyond the Ural Mountains that marked Europe's boundary with Asia. Still other stories told of sea monsters, horses with horns, and ants the size of dogs. Clearly, the world beyond Europe was an extremely dangerous place.

Some of these rumors had circulated in Europe ever since the days of the Romans. The classical historian Pliny the Elder, for instance, wrote about the mantichora, a creature that he confidently asserted made its home in Africa. The mantichora, Pliny reported, "has a triple row of teeth [and] the face and ears of a human being." It also had the sting of a scorpion and the body of a lion, along with—chillingly—"a special appetite for human flesh."[23] Where Pliny and other writers of the Roman era got their information is not entirely clear, but their ideas persisted well into the medieval period.

Other rumors were more recent. A few of these were probably exaggerated fact. With enough retellings, a report that a merchant had seen three or four unusually tall men in a land outside Europe could easily turn into a more distressing story about a squadron of giants. Some rumors, too, were deliberate fabrications. In the 1300s, for example, a man named John Mandeville wrote a book purporting to describe his journeys across the world. Most of the places he mentioned were entirely fictional, but Mandeville's descriptions of visits to alarming spots such as the Valley of the Devils provided Europeans with further evidence that the rest of the world was to be feared.

Like medieval conceptions of time, then, medieval images of the world echoed and shaped life during the Middle Ages. Because medieval Europe was an agricultural society, the people of the era naturally focused on the cycles of the seasons; this led to an understanding of time as endlessly repeating without evident forward motion. The emphasis on the holy days of the Christian Church served to underscore this idea; it also reflected the tremendous influence of Christianity on the people of medieval Europe. In the same way, medieval ideas of geography separated Europeans into small groups and pitted them against one another. Geographic understanding, or the lack of it, also supported the prevailing medieval notion that the world was to be mistrusted. Together, medieval concepts of time and space helped to form the mindset of the Middle Ages.

Chapter Three

AN ORDERED UNIVERSE

The notion of order was central to the medieval worldview. As the people of the Middle Ages saw it, the universe simply made sense. It had been created by God, the ultimate force of good, and it had been designed according to a grand plan. The rotation of the stars, the orbit of the sun, the hierarchy of the living things that populated the earth—all of these had been ordained by a rational God. The idea of an ordered universe was an extremely powerful one in medieval Europe. Like the standard Middle Ages ideas of time and space, the concept of order underlay the worldview of the period.

Creation

Like so much else in medieval Europe, the focus on order during the Middle Ages came in large part from the Bible. Specifically, it was rooted in the description of the Creation given in the first chapter of Genesis, the first book in the Old Testament. In this well-known account, God took six days to create the entire universe and all that was in it. First, he created light and separated the heavens from the earth. Later, God caused there to be water and dry land, the moon and the sun, and plants and animals. Finally, on the sixth day of creation, God made human beings. "Thus heaven and earth were completed with all their array [range of things]," reads Genesis 2:1.

In the Genesis account, creation was well ordered and enacted according to a grand plan. As Genesis described it, each day was reserved for a specific action. Each action, moreover, built on the ones before. There was not much point in having plants until there was a sun, after all, and little reason to create animals until there were plants for them to eat. Throughout the chapter, there is a sense of structure, order, and arrangement. As one biblical scholar puts it, the account "aims at a logical and exhaustive classification of beings."[24]

Nor was it any coincidence that the process culminated in the creation of humanity. According to Genesis, people held a special place in God's heart, for they were formed with their creator in mind. "Let us make man in our own image," God says in Genesis 1:27, "in the likeness of ourselves." In the biblical view, moreover, God gave humankind full dominion over the rest of creation.

God creates the world in this thirteenth-century fresco from Norway.

"Fill the earth and conquer it," God tells the first people, according to Genesis 1:28. "Be masters of the fish of the sea, the birds of heaven and all living animals on the earth." In this sense, the creation of humanity was the final piece in God's great plan.

"It Was Very Good"

The emphasis on order and reason in this account of the Creation struck a chord with medieval Europeans. To them, there was something compelling about the idea that the world had been created in a sensible and orderly way. Better yet, since the universe had been created by an all-good and all-powerful God, the universe had to be holy as well, for such a great being as God would not make something less than perfect in its design.

The holiness of the well-ordered universe was not mere theory. As Christians of the Middle Ages saw it, there was ample evidence for this view in the Bible. According to Genesis, they pointed out, God evaluated his work at the end of each day and found that it pleased him. After forming humankind, in particular, God took one final look at his creation. "God saw all he had made," reads Genesis 1:31, "and indeed it was very good." If God believed his creation was good, then it was not the business of mortals to argue.

Under these circumstances, it was impossible for medieval Europeans to believe that the universe had been anything short of ideal when it was first fashioned. "Everything was created by God," sums up Russell, "and, as God was immanent [always present] in the world, everything was an expression of God."[25] In this way, the entire universe could be seen as a faultless and sacred place. To the extent that the world as it existed was less than perfect, it was the fault of humanity. God had intended otherwise in his grand design, and creation was ample evidence of that.

Classical Ideas

Among the texts and ideas that predated the medieval period, the Bible was the strongest single influence during the Middle Ages. It was not, however, the only one. The Bible was rather silent on the question of the structure of the universe beyond Earth, for example. The creation account in Genesis 1 speaks vaguely of the "two great lights," the sun and the moon, and how God "set them in the vault of heaven" (Gen. 1:16–17). The specifics of this vault, evidently, were not of great interest to the authors of Genesis. For information on this subject, therefore, the people of the Middle Ages turned instead to the writings of the ancient Greeks and Romans.

In particular, they looked to the Greek scientist Ptolemy and his astronomical treatise the *Almagest*, published in 142. Ptolemy's conception of the cosmos, as expressed in the *Almagest*, was based on detailed study of the sky and the earth. It drew upon and extended the ideas of earlier thinkers, and in many ways it was a remarkable work. In particular, Ptolemy

Ptolemy, a second-century Greek astronomer, argued that Earth was at the center of the universe and did not rotate. His theories were accepted throughout the Middle Ages.

argued that Earth was stationary. As one historian notes, Ptolemy observed that "arrows shot straight up into the air fall directly back to Earth, whereas if the Earth rotated . . . the arrow should swerve in the direction opposite to the Earth's motion."[26] Ptolemy's conclusion carried the day, backed as it was by reason and careful observation, and the notion of a stationary Earth was widely accepted by Europeans until the very end of the Middle Ages.

More significantly, Ptolemy also assumed that Earth was at the very center of the universe. Once again, Ptolemy had good reasons for this judgment. Certainly, no observer could doubt that the sun, the moon, and the stars all appeared to orbit Earth. From a theological perspective, too, placing Earth in the middle of everything fit the biblical account of an Earth-centered creation that culminated in the rise of humanity. If Genesis was correct—and medieval Europeans firmly believed it was—then it was reasonable that all other stars and planets be subordinate to Earth and rotate around it.

The Rest of the Universe

Along with other classical thinkers, Ptolemy perceived great order in the cosmos. In his view, the universe was a series of spheres with Earth at their center.

brought mathematics to bear on the problem of how to describe the motion of heavenly bodies, most notably the planets, and his summation of the work of earlier thinkers is invaluable.

Nonetheless, the *Almagest* included two important mistakes. For one, Ptolemy

The Shape of the Earth

Ptolemy's errors in the *Almagest* did not include a belief that Earth was flat. Like other classical scholars, he knew better. Although at the time, of course, no one had risen above Earth's surface to verify that the planet was round, it was nonetheless clear to educated Greeks and Romans that a flat Earth was impossible. Evidence for this came from several sources, but particularly from two observations in everyday life. For one, during a lunar eclipse Earth casts a round shadow against the moon. For another, people standing on a beach could see the mast of an approaching sailing ship before the rest of the ship became visible. Both these arguments were known to the ancient Greeks and Romans; both were compelling evidence that Earth is a globe. Ptolemy incorporated the notion of a round Earth into the *Almagest*. Educated medieval thinkers agreed with his argument. The idea of a round Earth, then, was widely accepted among the scholars of the Middle Ages.

Closest to Earth was the sphere that contained the moon. Beyond that came another sphere, this one encompassing the sun. The distance between the two spheres guaranteed that sun and moon would never collide. The stars were farther back still, rotating on a distant sphere of their own. As for the planets, their often erratic motion was a puzzle, but classical astronomers finally concluded that each planet occupied its own sphere; the explanation was a bit inelegant, but it was as good an explanation as any.

Medieval Europeans largely accepted the theories of Ptolemy and other classical astronomers. However, the people of the Middle Ages supplemented classical astronomy with religious ideas drawn from Christianity. As Ptolemy and the other ancients saw it, for example, the stars formed the sphere most distant from Earth. The medieval Christians, however, added a new sphere beyond the stars: heaven. "The outermost layer of all consisted of the heavens created by God on the first day," sums up historian Charles Freeman. "Ptolemy's works were thus absorbed into a Christian cosmology."[27]

The addition of heaven to Ptolemy's original scheme not only incorporated Christian doctrine into the medieval worldview, it also further underscored the medieval passion for order. Even more than the classical version of the cosmos, the medieval conception of the

Pictured is a fifteenth-century representation of the Ptolemaic system of the cosmos. Earth is at the center as other planets revolve around it.

universe followed a systematic progression. As medieval thinkers saw it, each successive sphere was more pure and godly than the one before it. "Moving away from the earth," writes Freeman, "from the moon to the planets and then to the . . . stars, each sphere was closer to 'the unchanging,' with heaven, the ultimate immutable [unchanging] sphere, lying beyond."[28]

The medieval image of the cosmos clearly reflected the era's focus on pattern and design. In an uncertain world where dangers lurked at every turn, it was comforting to think that the stars, at least, were fixed in their own assigned sphere, that the sun would rise each morning, and that the universe had been created in a grand and wonderful way by a good and powerful God. During the six days of the Creation, medieval Europeans believed, God had put the stars, the planets, the sun, and the moon in their places and set them all in motion. There they would stay, following predictable courses, until God himself chose to remove them—that is, until the end of time.

Order on Earth

The medieval emphasis on order and logic was also apparent in the way the people of the Middle Ages thought about God and the natural world he had called into being on earth. Just as the stars and the planets had their places in the sky, reasoned medieval Europeans, so must each living thing have its

own place and its own purpose. For that matter, so did the angels, the heavenly assistants who helped God carry out his grand plan. As the medieval Europeans saw it, every aspect of the created world, seen and unseen, was a manifestation of the care and order with which God had organized the world.

Once again, the basis for this idea can be seen in the Bible. As chapter 1 of Genesis explains, the first living things were plants. Next, God continued by fashioning the birds and "every kind of living creature with which the waters teem" (Gen. 1:21). After forming these creatures, God added reptiles, cattle, and other land animals. Finally, he created humankind. The progression of the Creation seemed perfectly logical to medieval Europeans. God began with silent, immobile, unthinking plants, and worked his way up to human beings: mobile and intelligent, capable of speech, and made in the image of God himself.

The medieval mind viewed the hierarchy of beings on earth in precisely this way. Humans, of course, ranked at the top. "Of all material creatures," writes Russell, summing up the medieval perspective, "[humans] are the most spiritual. Because they alone of earthly creatures have self-knowledge and a comprehension of good and evil, they [alone] have an immortal soul."[29] This capacity to

God creates the animals in this twelfth-century painting. Medieval Europeans reasoned that every living thing had its purpose in the world.

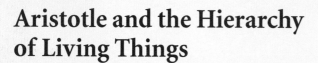

Aristotle and the Hierarchy of Living Things

The hierarchy of living things is not only a Christian idea. It also appears in classical thought. The Greek philosopher Aristotle, for example, developed a hierarchy of his own, similar in most respects to the inverted order of the Creation. Like the Bible, Aristotle gave humans primacy in his hierarchy, but his reasoning was slightly different. To him, the distinction between humans and other animals was not that humans had immortal souls or that they were made in the image of God; instead, it was simply that he believed humans to be the only beings capable of rational thought. Medieval scholars most likely drew on the ideas of Aristotle as well as on biblical imagery to formulate their notion of the hierarchy of living things.

make choices, to live a life of understanding, separated human beings from the lesser forms of life that populated the earth—and put them on the highest level of all living things.

Lower Levels

Medieval thinkers believed, however, that the lower creatures had a hierarchy of their own. Ranking immediately below humans were the animals, generally arranged on several levels according to their perceived level of intelligence. Monkeys and other primates, though not widespread in Europe, were at the top of the animal hierarchy, due in large part to the obvious similarities they showed with humans. Cats, dogs, horses, cattle, and other large mammals appeared slightly lower on the list. They in turn were followed by small mammals, reptiles, birds, and fish. Below these, at last, came the plant kingdom.

The notion of a hierarchy of living things had clear connections with the Creation described in the book of Genesis. In some ways, in fact, the medieval hierarchy of life is nothing more than the order of the Creation inverted and slightly expanded. Humans are at the top of the hierarchy because they can think and make choices and because they have an immortal soul; but mostly because in the biblical account of the Creation, humans are made in the image of God and given dominion over the rest of the world.

The medieval conception of a hierarchy of beings did not remain static through the medieval period, however. Saint Thomas Aquinas, who lived during the 1200s, extended and refined the notion by theorizing that the lower ranks of the hierarchy existed only for the purposes of the ranks that came above them. Thus, it was acceptable—even expected—for a person to ride a horse, milk a cow, or eat a pig; in the same way, carnivorous animals ate smaller animals, and herbivores ate plants. As Aquinas and other late medieval thinkers described it, then, this hierarchy was truly the natural order of the world.

Order in Heaven

To medieval thinkers, there was not only an earthly hierarchy, but a celestial, or heavenly, one as well. The top of the celestial hierarchy was, of course, God.

Cherubim, angels of high rank, surround Jesus in this fourteenth-century church mosaic.

Below him were his angels, who communicated on God's behalf with people on earth and fulfilled other functions in God's heavenly kingdom. "As disembodied voices or full-bodied messengers," notes one author, pointing out the prevalence of angels in Christian thought and imagery, "angels float through more than half the books of the Bible."[30]

Simply placing God above the angels, though, was not enough for the people of the Middle Ages. In keeping with the general view that rank and order appeared everywhere, medieval scholars argued that even the angels had a hierarchy of their own—a hierarchy of remarkable complexity. These ideas came originally from a book called *The Celestial Hierarchy*, which was published around 500 and probably written by a Syrian monk. Based on the conclusions of this book, medieval scholars divided the angels into three general groups, each with three subgroups—a total of nine classes of angels in all.

At the top of the hierarchy were the seraphim, the cherubim, and the thrones. These three angel subgroups most closely resembled God and spent all their time quite literally singing God's praises in heaven. The second triad included three groups who divided their time between heaven and earth; the virtues, for example, were believed to heal people who were sick, while the dominions served as what Panati describes as "celestial

Satan and the Angels

The one being that did not fit easily into medieval hierarchies was Satan. According to medieval theology and Christian tradition, Satan was originally an angel. However, he chose to reject God and instead do battle with the powers of good. Ejected from heaven, he and his followers—angels turned demons—traveled to hell and began to create an empire of evil. "Better to reign in hell," the poet John Milton imagined Satan saying, "than serve in heaven."

Satan was typically seen as more powerful than an ordinary angel; his strength and influence, indeed, ranked second only to God's. On the other hand, Satan was much weaker than it might have appeared. He lacked the blessing and authority that God extended to the angel host in heaven, and as theologians saw it, Satan was doomed to lose the cosmic struggle with God in the end. Thus, most Christian thinkers of the Middle Ages saw Satan as standing apart from the celestial hierarchy—not as powerful as God, certainly, but not truly comparable with the angels either.

Quoted in Charles Panati, *Sacred Origins of Profound Things*. New York: Penguin, 1996, p. 365.

housekeepers."[31] Finally, the lowest triad consisted of the angels whose work was mainly carried out on earth. This class included messenger angels such as Gabriel, who according to the New Testament informed Mary that she would give birth to Jesus.

Thus, medieval thinkers agreed that all the beings of the universe, those on earth as well as those in heaven, had their place in an ordered hierarchy. In the medieval cosmology, this hierarchy stretched from God, the supreme ruler of the entire cosmos, down through angels, humans, animals, and finally down to the lowliest flowers and trees. The medieval passion for order gave each cow, each seraph, and each human being its own well-defined role in the grand plan of the universe, just as it had given each star and each planet its own specific course in the sky.

This focus on order underlay much of the philosophy of the Middle Ages. The universe, in this view, was not random or arbitrary; instead, it was sensible, logical, and above all, created as an extension of God's own goodness. At its heart, then, the world was intended to be a just and kind place. This image of a rational, untainted world carried great power among Europeans of the medieval period; to a very large degree, indeed, it formed a central focus of the medieval worldview. The certainty that there was a fundamental order to the workings of the entire universe offered comfort to medieval Europeans and helped them keep their hope and faith when life on earth became difficult to bear.

Chapter Four

A DISORDERLY WORLD

The people of the Middle Ages firmly believed that God had created the universe to be a pure and orderly place. The world inhabited by medieval Europeans, however, fell considerably short of perfection. The Europe of the Middle Ages was harsh and violent. Droughts, storms, and deadly epidemics were evidence of the cruelties of nature. The prevalence of war, crime, and poverty, in turn, suggested that humans were no kinder to one another. If there was indeed a grand plan to the universe, it was much easier to glimpse in the movements of the distant stars or in the ranks of the celestial angels than it was by searching the streets of Paris or the manors along the Rhine.

Medieval Europeans were well aware of the gap between the world they believed God had created and the world as it actually appeared. They strove to restore God's great design by making the impure, disorderly, and corrupted earth a reflection of the splendid order of the cosmos. In the long run, of course, this struggle was doomed to failure. But the attempt to restore perfection shaped medieval society in several important ways and had an enormous impact on the medieval way of thinking. Like the notion of an ordered universe, the image of a disorderly earth colored the way medieval Europeans perceived their lives and the world around them.

Disaster and Violence

There is no question that life during the Middle Ages could be grim. For one thing, it was short. Pope Boniface VIII, who held office in the 1300s, lived to be well over eighty, but he was a notable exception in those difficult times. Although reliable statistics are hard to come by, some historians think that life expectancy during much of the medieval period may have been as low as twenty-five. It is doubtful that life expectancy ever exceeded thirty-five in any part of Europe at any point during the Middle Ages.

The reasons for early death were many. Women succumbed to the stresses of childbirth; babies, whose immune systems were not well developed, sickened and died before they reached their first birthdays. Peasants died of overwork and poor nutrition, their bodies weakened and aged before they reached the age of fifty. Famine, caused by drought, heavy rains, or bitter cold, swept through Europe periodically, taking tens or hundreds of thousands of lives at once. In 1356 a violent earthquake struck Switzerland, destroying virtually the entire city of Basel and many settlements nearby.

Wars were another problem. The Middle Ages were marked by frequent battles of great destructiveness. About four thousand French knights died in the Battle of Crécy in 1346, for instance. At least two European wars during this period lasted, on and off, for more than a century. And, of course, medieval warfare affected not just soldiers, but also the

A Belgian painting depicts the Black Death, a plague that killed 20 million Europeans in the 1300s.

The Black Death

The following excerpt is from an account written by Agnolo di Tura, an Italian living in Siena when the Black Death struck in 1348.

It was a cruel and horrible thing, and I do not know where to begin to tell of the cruelty and the pitiless ways. It seemed to almost everyone that one became stupefied by seeing the pain. And it is impossible for the human tongue to recount the awful thing. Indeed one who did not see such horribleness can be called blessed. And the victims died almost immediately. They would swell beneath their armpits and in their groins, and fall over dead while talking. Father abandoned child, wife husband, one brother another; for this illness seemed to strike through the breath and sight. And soon they died. And none could be found to bury the dead for money or friendship. . . . And in many places in Siena great pits were dug and piled deep with the multitude of dead. And they died by the hundreds both day and night, and all were thrown in these ditches and covered over with earth. And as soon as these ditches were filled more were dug.

Quoted in Norman F. Cantor, *The Medieval Reader.* New York: HarperCollins, 1994, pp. 280–81.

peasants of the countryside and the people of the cities. All too often, fighting disrupted food supplies, displaced civilians, and destroyed entire communities.

The most alarming source of death in medieval Europe, however, was disease. Epidemics struck suddenly and apparently without warning, and at their worst they were extraordinarily destructive. The worst of all was the Black Death, probably the bubonic plague, which attacked virtually all of Europe in 1347—and reappeared several more times during the period as well. The number of deaths due to this outbreak is uncertain, but modern scholarship tends to agree with Froissart's offhand lament that "a third of the world died."[32] Within Europe, that would have meant a death toll of about 20 million people.

"Less than a Pittance"

The violence of the world revealed itself in more than death. Those who survived plagues and other epidemics, for example, were often weakened, scarred, or otherwise disfigured. Even those who escaped infection had to survive the trauma

Medieval farmers were usually unable to produce enough food for themselves, which made them constantly hungry and susceptible to disease.

of burying family members and friends. One Italian chronicler, who lost all five of his children to the Black Death, started to describe the epidemic's effects in an account written some time afterward, but he found himself emotionally unable to put his ideas into words. "It was all so horrible that I, the writer," he explained, "cannot think of it and so will not continue."[33]

Even in times without plague or outright famine, medieval Europeans frequently suffered. Near-constant hunger, for example, was a reality for quite a few peasants. No matter how hard they worked, most farmers were seldom able to produce all the food they needed. Just a few days of unfavorable weather at the wrong time could destroy enough crops to create a serious shortage of food. A poet of the 1300s lamented the fate of the rural poor, who had "full many to feed and few pence to do it," and who could offer their families only "bread and penny-ale that is less than a pittance."[34]

The lack of sufficient food pointed up a problem in medieval society: the imbalance in resources. For every well-fed, well-off nobleman there were dozens, perhaps hundreds, of peasants barely able to make ends meet, and the economic policies of medieval Europe tended to support this inequality. Peasants were taxed heavily by the lords who ruled them, and they were often forbidden to seek a new life elsewhere. From time to time, peasants staged rebellions, and some thinkers of the time took their side. "Ye nobles are like ravening wolves," complained one author of the 1200s, "who despoil your subjects and live on the blood and sweat of the poor."[35]

The Fall

Social discord, starvation, disease, warfare—the world of the Middle Ages was clearly very far from the sacred, perfect place that Christians believed God had created it to be. In Christian doctrine, the reason for this discord could be found in the book of Genesis. According to the second chapter of this book, God planted a garden in a place called Eden and turned it into an earthly paradise for the use of Adam and Eve, the first two human beings. In this account, God told Adam that the pair could eat the fruit of any tree in the garden but one. That was the fruit of the tree of "the knowledge of good and evil" (Gen. 2:17). Adam and Eve, God explained, were not to touch the fruit of this tree under any circumstances.

But Adam and Eve did not obey God's instructions. According to the narrative, Satan, in the guise of a serpent, tempted Eve to pick and eat the fruit of this tree and then to feed it to her husband. By eating the fruit, the two gained self-awareness and the knowledge of good and evil. At the same time, they incurred the wrath of God. To punish their disobedience, God evicted Adam and Eve from the garden and forced them to make their own way in the world, thus exposing them to pain, toil, and the prospect of death. "With sweat on your brow shall you eat your bread," God tells Adam in Genesis 3:19, "until you return to the soil. . . . For dust you are and to dust you shall return."

Like the rest of the Bible, this narrative —often known as the Fall of Adam—

Adam and Eve are banished from Paradise in this thirteenth-century manuscript. People of the Middle Ages believed that they too were condemned to pay for Adam and Eve's sin.

was taken literally by virtually all Christians in medieval Europe. To the people of the Middle Ages, the Fall explained the sorry state of humanity. By disobeying God, Adam and Eve had brought sin into the world and permanently cut themselves off from earthly paradise. Their decision to eat the fruit had ruined the happy, if ignorant, life of leisure they had enjoyed. And because God's condemnation applied not only to Adam and Eve but also to their descendants, all generations of humankind were now subject to the sufferings of an imperfect world.

Thus medieval thinkers blamed humankind, not God, for the dismal state of the world around them. The sins of Adam and Eve had brought on God's angry yet justifiable response. "We made our choice in Adam," writes Russell in summarizing the medieval perspective, "and we are therefore inherently corrupt. . . . It is not God who has condemned man but man who has damned himself."[36]

Punishment and Affliction

For the people of the Middle Ages, moreover, God was still angry at humanity for Adam and Eve's disobedience. Thus, medieval Europeans tended to see God's handiwork in the disasters that befell the world. They largely rejected the notion that calamity was caused by

Pope Clement VI (center) believed God was punishing Christians by afflicting them with the Black Death.

random forces of nature, believing instead that all natural catastrophes were willed by God as punishment for human behavior. "There is a certain heresy concerning earthquakes that they come not from God's command," complained one early Christian thinker, "but [instead] from the very nature of the elements."[37] As the writer's use of the word "heresy" suggests, this notion was never widespread during the Middle Ages; most people readily accepted that

earthquakes, like other disasters, did indeed arise from "God's command."

Evidence of this acceptance is easy to find in the writings of the Middle Ages. A poem about a famine that struck much of northern Europe in the early 1300s, for example, explained that God had made the weather "so cold and unkynde"[38] that crops could not grow. The reason, the poet continued, was to punish humans for the sin of pride. Only by honest repentance, in this view, would the famine come to an end. This perspective echoed several fundamental medieval beliefs: that the universe was ordered, even if the world was not; that God had a grand plan and a reason for all he did; and that human behavior, more than anything else, was what kept the world in disarray.

The Black Death, too, was widely seen as a punishment. Few medieval thinkers perceived the plague as an arbitrary event. Pope Clement VI spoke for many in 1348 when he referred to the "pestilence with which God is afflicting the Christian people."[39] Frantic with fear and worry, Europeans appealed to God for relief from the epidemic. Theories abounded as to what humans might have done to bring on such a ghastly expression of God's fury. Many writers suggested that the culprit was greed. Others pointed toward lust, mistreatment of the poor, or failure to observe all the rules of the church, among many others. Few, however, disputed the central notion that God had deliberately sent the plague to punish humanity.

The Search for Order

In this way, the disorder of the everyday world was the logical result of human misbehavior, both during the Fall and during the medieval period itself. The people of the Middle Ages, however, did their best to restore the perfection and order that God had intended. They did this by establishing rigid social and

Good, Better, Excellent

Some writers of the medieval era were so concerned with finding order that they devised rankings within rankings. Among these was Abbon of Fleury, a French monk in the late 900s who championed the value of monks as compared to other clergymen in this excerpt:

Among Christians . . . we know well that there exist three orders [that is, groups] and, so to speak, three levels. The first is that of the laity [lay people, or those who were not monks or priests], the second that of the clergy [used in this case to mean priests as distinct from monks], the third that of the monks. Although none of the three is exempt from sin, the first is good, the second is better, and the third is excellent.

Abbon also worked out the ratio of monks, priests, and lay people in heaven, which he took to be ten monks for every six priests and three lay people. What the priests and lay people thought of his calculations—and his overall argument—does not seem to have been recorded.

Quoted in Jacques Le Goff, ed., *The Medieval World.* London: Parkgate, 1997, pp. 53–54.

political systems that mirrored the tidy hierarchies of creation and the cosmos. Medieval thinkers conceded that the people of Europe could never re-create the blissful world before the Fall. Still, it was possible to construct a world that was patterned after the neatly ordered universe, and the people of the Middle Ages threw themselves eagerly into this task.

The structure of the church, of course, was one obvious way in which medieval Europeans mirrored the carefully ordered hierarchies of heaven and living creatures. As historian Norman Cantor puts it, the medieval church had a "vision of churchmen rightfully dictating to laity [ordinary churchgoers], and bishops and abbots dictating to ordinary priests, monks, and nuns, and the pope in Rome as the Vicar of Christ dictating to everybody."[40] Bishop and archbishop, priest and monk—each had his own place in the pyramid. A bishop was to a priest much as an angel was to a human or as a sheep was to a flower. In this way, the hierarchical church structure matched the image medieval Europeans had regarding God's greater creation.

Feudalism

The political and economic structure of the Middle Ages also attempted to create a more orderly society even in the midst of disaster and disease. The basic social system used during medieval times was known as feudalism, which rested on an agreement between poor peasants, or serfs, and a much wealthier nobleman. Under the feudal system, noblemen offered land and protection to serfs. In exchange, serfs agreed to share their crop yields with their lords, to serve as soldiers, and to carry out other tasks as necessary. "Throughout the year he shall work every second day," reads a description of a serf's responsibilities on an English manor in 1298, "carrying or mowing or reaping or carting, or doing some other work according as his lord commands him."[41]

The details of feudalism differed according to time and place. Like the church, however, feudalism everywhere formed a hierarchy. At the top of the pyramid were emperors and kings— leaders who ruled enormous territories. The nobles who controlled the manors ranked below royalty, but considerably above the merchants and other members of the small urban middle class of the time. The middle class, in turn, outranked the serfs, who made up 98 percent of the population by some modern estimates but were nonetheless at the bottom of the social structure.

Nor did feudalism allow much change in class status. The church did provide some opportunity for the sons of peasants to get an education and become monks, priests, perhaps even bishops. But since the clergy was celibate, a

A fifteenth-century depiction of feudalism shows peasants vowing their allegiance to their lord's magistrate.

Omme par la vertu de pruden ce qui entre bie & mal subtille ment considere et conchnoist humain couraige & entende ment soit informe & enseigne de la conchnoissance du bien prouffitable et dele table & ammie et meu a la

poursuiure. Et es biens terrie tresdouly estat prouffitable plaisant & delectable paisible & ordonne soit clerment trou ue par raison on lun dout bien querir de bon cuer selon ce que len puet. Et quant il est trouue bien dert comme tresor inestimable & precieuy en grat humilite et patience diligen

Sacred Kingship

The relative status of kings and popes in medieval Europe was the subject of considerable debate. In part this was a political discussion, but it was also theological. The issue centered on the question of sacred kingship—whether kings drew their power from divine support. Popes, predictably, sought to downplay sacred kingship and argued that popes always outranked kings. Pope Gregory VII, in fact, issued a document to this effect in the 1000s.

Not everyone agreed with Gregory, however, especially in the case of powerful and charismatic kings. The great emperor Charlemagne, for instance, was seen as very close to divine by many of his people. As one cleric told Charle-magne, "You are the avenger of crimes, you are the guide of the erring, you are the consoler of the grieving, you are the exaltation of good men. . . . Nothing can be concealed from your wisdom." And an anonymous archbishop wrote a treatise that supported the general idea of sacred kingship, regardless of who held the throne. "No one receives greater or better blessings," he wrote of kings, "or is consecrated and dedicated to God with greater or higher sacraments, not even indeed with as many and equal sacraments, and because of this no one is the king's equal."

Quoted in Norman F. Cantor, *The Medieval Reader.* New York: HarperCollins, 1994, pp. 104, 105.

---

peasant-turned-priest could not pass this new social rank on to the next generation. And apart from the church, feudal society was remarkably static. There was essentially no way for a serf to become a noble. Even movement in and out of the middle class was relatively rare. As medieval Europeans saw it, every person, like every star and every angel, had his or her individual role to play. "A carpenter ought not to try to become a knight," Russell writes, summing up the prevailing medieval attitude; "on the other hand, no one ought to deprive him of his proper status as a carpenter."[42]

Thus, the medieval worldview encompassed two quite different and contradictory ideas regarding the state of the world and the universe beyond it. On the one hand, the people of the Middle Ages believed that God had created a universe that was both organized and benevolent. From the movement of the stars to the relationship among the various species of animals, everything had its own rank and order and everything followed a predictable pattern. As medieval Europeans knew well, God had looked upon his creation and found it good.

Yet the sad reality was that medieval Europeans were scarcely strangers to hunger, disease, warfare, and other catastrophes. Much as these people wished to live in a world with the optimism and order of the one God had created, they knew they did not—and they believed they had only themselves and their ancestors to blame. Under these circumstances, the desire to return to an ordered existence, to restore the pattern and sense of the original creation, was powerful for medieval Europeans. And they worked hard to create whatever order they could within the institutions that made up their disorderly world.

Chapter Five

MIRACLES, PRAYERS, AND RELICS

The people of medieval Europe had very little control over the world around them. Farmers were at the mercy of the weather, merchants at risk of a disruption in trade routes. There was no telling when wars or epidemics might break out. The world, in short, was unpredictable and often unsafe. A favorite image during the Middle Ages, in fact, was the wheel of fortune—a representation of a constantly spinning wheel or globe, arbitrarily "carrying societies and individuals up to success or down to ruin,"[43] as historian Jacques Roussiaud puts it.

Europeans of the medieval period recognized this lack of control—and sought desperately to overcome it. All through the Middle Ages, the people of western Europe struggled to gain a sense of power over the random world that surrounded them. The hierarchical structures of the church and the feudal system were in part attempts to impose order on a world apparently ruled by chance. At the same time, though, medieval Europeans also tried to influence events by imploring God to intervene on their behalf. The certainty that God could intervene in such a way—and the possibility that he would—formed an important part of the medieval worldview.

Prayer

Prayer, or communication with God, was central to the Christian faith, and most medieval Christians took prayer quite seriously. This was especially true of nuns and monks. The single most important task of these people was prayer;

A man and his wife take time to pray. Medieval Christians took prayer very seriously as a way to communicate with God.

indeed, convents and monasteries were originally designed to be quiet places, removed from the everyday world, where frequent prayer was truly possible. Nearly all monks and nuns of the Middle Ages followed a precise schedule in which they repeated prayers at various intervals throughout the day. Some monks and nuns, indeed, spent most of their waking hours engaged in prayer.

But ordinary Christians of the time prayed, too, and by all accounts they did so frequently. Many medieval Europeans followed the instruction of the apostle Paul, given in 1 Thessalonians 5:17, to "pray without ceasing." Certainly, prayer was considered a sign of piety and holiness. That was true in the everyday world; it was also true in the fiction of the period. The German epic poem the *Nibelungenlied*, for instance, informs readers that the character Kriemhild never missed morning prayer —a fact that stands as an illustration of her essential goodness.

Several Forms of Prayer

Within the Christian tradition, prayer could take several forms. Many prayers were prayers of thanksgiving, or gratefulness. Others were prayers of confession, used to expunge sins and apologize for wrongdoing. "Have mercy on me, O God, in your goodness," reads the first verse of Psalm 51; "in your great tenderness wipe away my faults." Still other prayers expressed adoration of God or praised him and his works. "I shall im-

mortalize your name," says Psalm 45:17; "nations will sing your praises for ever and ever."

All of these forms of prayer were used by medieval Christians. The form that was most frequent during the Middle Ages, however, was the prayer of petition, in which a person begged God for help or for favor. Petitional prayers reflect a universal human need—the hope for assistance in time of want—and they were certainly not unique to medieval Christianity. The prayer of petition is found in all religions and all cultures, and is, in a sense, the most basic of all the varieties of prayer. "In all likelihood," theorizes Panati, "the very first human prayer fervently uttered was a cry for help—a petitional prayer."[44]

There were specific reasons, however, why the petitional prayer was so central to the medieval world. One, quite simply, was the dismal state of medieval Europe. The Middle Ages were a period of strife and struggle, a time when human beings seemed to teeter constantly on the brink of disaster. Wars, plagues, hard work, droughts—all made life grim and often overwhelming. Medieval Europeans, then, had many reasons to implore God to take pity on them and improve their lives.

The agricultural basis of medieval civilization also helped make prayers of petition particularly common in the Middle Ages. In a primitive farm society such as medieval Europe, the entire food supply depended on the weather—a variable completely outside human control. Any

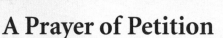

A Prayer of Petition

The Dies Irae—*Latin for "Day of Wrath"—was one of the great hymns created during the Middle Ages. This hymn text described the coming Day of Judgment, when people would be divided into the sheep—an image describing those who would be given eternal life with God—and the goats, who would be condemned to the flames of hell. Much of the text is actually a prayer of petition, as the following excerpt indicates:*

Though unworthy my petition, Grant me full and free remission [forgiveness], And redeem me from perdition [hell]. Be my lot on love decreed me: From the goats in safety lead me; With thy sheep forever feed me. When thy foes are all confounded, And with bitter flames surrounded, Call me to thy bliss unbounded. From the dust I pray thee, hear me: When my end shall come, be near me; Let thy grace sustain and cheer me.

Quoted in Norman F. Cantor, *The Medieval Reader.* New York: HarperCollins, 1994, p. 179.

---

unseasonable weather conditions, from heavy autumn rains to cold spring nights, could ruin the entire harvest in a given area and sometimes destroy the crops in an area tens of thousands of miles square. The resulting loss of crops devastated not only farmers, but nobles and city dwellers, too. "The whole world was troubled,"[45] wrote one chronicler of a widespread famine in 1316.

To some degree, food shortages could be made up through trade or by carefully storing crops from good years to use in lean ones. Moreover, when crops failed in a limited region, those affected by the resulting famine could sometimes migrate to other areas where conditions were more favorable. But these measures could not make up for widespread crop failures. Furthermore, trade was time consuming, crop storage was expensive, and migration often led to warfare. "Inhabitants in the new areas," notes one historian, "were loath to allow strangers to work the land and strain their resources."[46]

Help from God

If there were no good human solutions to the problem of famine—and it seemed there were not—then the only possible way to influence events was to appeal to God. As a result, the people of the Middle Ages frequently petitioned God to give them abundant harvests and good weather. They prayed for rain when the days had been dry and for sun when the fields had become soaked. They begged for enough to eat, not just on a given

Domine ne in furore
tuo arguas me: ne
$\mathfrak{g}$ in ira tua corripi
as me.

day or in a given week, but throughout an entire year. The line "Give us this day our daily bread," from the Lord's Prayer (Matt. 6:11), has lost its impact for many well-fed Christians of modern America. To medieval Europeans, however, the prayer was a deeply sincere and vital request: a prayer of petition.

Asking God to intervene made perfect sense according to the medieval worldview. God, after all, was fundamentally in charge of everything. He had set the planets in their orbits; he had summoned the earth into being; he had created the entire hierarchy of life from the lowliest insect to humanity itself. Medieval thinkers did not suppose that God had designed the world and then stepped aside to let it run like a giant clock or mill wheel, an idea that became popular some centuries afterward. Instead, they believed God was still very active in his creation and deeply engaged with his people.

To petition God for rain, sun, or warmth, then, was reasonable, for God controlled the weather, just as he controlled every other aspect of life on earth. If God was angry at humanity, he would send unfavorable weather, dooming crops to failure and people to starvation. The disobedience of Adam and Eve had given God cause for anger.

King David of Israel (bottom) looks to God for a blessing in this fifteenth-century manuscript. Christians believed prayer could bring order to society and the world.

Only prayer—honest, sincere prayer—might suffice to get him to relax that resentment, if only for a day, a month, or a season. Similar reasoning led medieval Europeans to pray not just for favorable weather, but for other gifts as well: victory in battle, successful transactions in business, and—perhaps most of all—good health.

Indeed, though prayers for good harvests may have been more common, prayers to keep away the wrath of pestilence were perhaps even more fervent. This was particularly true at the time of the Black Death. Across Europe, church leaders organized mass prayer processions and vigils in which hundreds of people implored God to spare them and their communities from the ravages of the plague. Pope Clement VI even declared 1348 to be a holy year, in which Christians were asked to come to Rome to take part in prayer meetings to convince God to bring an end to the dying.

These prayer meetings were singularly unsuccessful. Most were counterproductive as well; the large crowds present at these events hastened the spread of the germs that caused the deaths. Some Europeans, despairing of ever gaining God's good graces, gave up on prayer altogether. "God is dead now-a-days and deigneth not hear us," wrote poet William Langland, speaking for many, "and prayers have no power the Plague to stay [keep away]."[47] Others, however, continued to pray. In their view, God remained the only possible solution to the dreadful pestilence.

Saints

To medieval Europeans, God was the ultimate authority—certainly the only being capable of changing the weather or ending a plague. But most prayers of petition during the Middle Ages were not offered directly to God. God was widely seen as distant, difficult to comprehend, and swift to anger. Many medieval Europeans found it hard to imagine that God would listen to their prayers—or that he would choose to carry out their wishes if he did.

For most medieval Europeans, then, the solution was to pray to intermediaries—beings who, in effect, carry the prayers of others to God. Given a remote and possibly hostile God, it made sense for medieval Christians to bring their concerns to what Panati calls "someone already pure and conveniently close to [God] in Heaven."[48] Of course, no living person fit that description; heaven, after all, was reserved for people who had died. Fortunately for the people of the Middle Ages, though, one category of being did combine purity with closeness to God: the saints of the church.

Saints were people who had died after having done great things for their Christian faith. Some had been great scholars, mystics, or prophets. Others had tirelessly spread the Christian message. Many more had been martyred, killed because they professed Christianity. Polycarp, a second-century bishop, for example, was ordered by a Roman official to reject Jesus. When Polycarp refused, saying, "I have served him [Jesus] for eighty-six years and he has done me no wrong,"[49] he was burned alive. Whether martyrs or not, however, all saints had led lives that were exemplary.

Miracles

Nearly all saints were associated with miracles, defined by Saint Augustine as events "in contradiction to that which is known to us of nature."[50] According to the Bible, Jesus had performed a number of great miracles: casting out demons, healing the sick, calming storms, and much more. In theory at least, every saint was supposed to have emulated Jesus by performing miracles during his or her lifetime. Many of these miracles, though not all, involved healing those who appeared to be permanently ill. Acts 8:7, for instance, describes Saint Philip's miraculous ability to cure "paralytics and cripples" soon after the death of Jesus.

The specifics of many miracles were lost in legend, especially for the earliest of the saints, and may well have been embellished as time went on. "A high degree of authenticity and historical fact is a rather rare element" in the stories of early saints, writes Donald Attwater, the author of a dictionary of saints. Instead, he notes, many of these tales are filled with "myth, folklore, legend, and romantic and edifying fiction."[51] Still, the

According to legend, St. Catherine of Alexandria was martyred for spreading the word of Christianity. She is pictured here with the wheel on which she was tortured.

The Miracles of the Virgin

The Miracles of the Virgin was a collection of stories about the Virgin Mary, Jesus's mother, and the miracles that she had performed over the years. First published in the 1100s, the book soon became quite popular in western Europe. Its popularity persisted for the rest of the medieval era.

The miracles described in the book did not come only to people who had led good and largely blameless lives. Instead, the bulk of these miracles were performed for people whose lives had been less than exemplary. To the Mary depicted in the book, what mattered most was the devotion people showed to her.

One tale, for instance, told of a thief named Eddo, who, in the words of historian R.W. Southern, "was in the habit of saluting [Mary] even on his marauding expeditions." Caught and hanged, Eddo nevertheless did not die. Instead, Southern continues, "the Virgin held him up for two days, and when his executioners tried to fix the rope more tightly, she put her hands to his throat and prevented them." In the end, Eddo was set free.

Quoted in R. W. Southern, *The Making of the Middle Ages.* New Haven, CT: Yale University Press, 1953, p. 249

people of the Middle Ages believed absolutely in the fact of the miracles, even if details of each event were sometimes uncertain.

Medieval Europeans, moreover, believed that miracles were present in their own world. No matter how ill a person became, there was always the chance of a complete and miraculous recovery—a true gift from God. Miracles could take other forms, too. In 1224, as a biographer reported, the mystic Saint Francis of Assisi saw "a seraph with six shining, fiery wings descend from heaven."[52] Suddenly, Francis developed open wounds on his hands, feet, and side in the precise spots where Jesus had supposedly been wounded while on the cross. Francis believed that the wounds and the vision of the seraph were part of a miracle that served to draw him closer to Jesus.

Intermediaries and Patron Saints

The saints had been real people—exceptionally good people, perhaps, but people nevertheless. As a result, medieval

Apollonia became the patron saint of people who suffered from toothaches because all of her teeth were knocked out during her martyrdom.

Christians believed that the saints understood human worries and complaints. Mary, the mother of Jesus, for example, "knew what it was like to suffer bereavement and loss," writes Russell. "She could sympathize with the sufferings of poor mortals."[53] The saints were therefore not only favored by God but well disposed to listen to human prayers. Consequently, the people of the Middle Ages flooded the saints with prayers, begging them to pass their petitions on to God.

In theory, almost any saint would do as an intermediary. However, some saints came to be seen as especially well suited for the role. Mary was a particular favorite, and many medieval Europeans reported great results when addressing prayers to her. In one case reported by a chronicler of the time, a young boy had been blinded by a thorn that had penetrated his eye. When his mother prayed to Mary, however, a great miracle took place. As the chronicler described it, "The thorn falls out, the inflammation disappears, and the mother returns home with her son no longer blind."[54] Similar stories involving Mary were widespread throughout Europe.

Other saints, known as patron saints, were especially inclined to answer the prayers of certain groups of people—notably those with a specific disease or those who held a certain occupation. When Saint Apollonia was martyred, for example, all of her teeth were knocked out. As a result, she was the patron saint of people who suffered from toothaches. "Having suffered through this torment," writes historian Paul B. Newman, "[Apollonia] was believed to be especially sympathetic towards others who were suffering similar problems."[55] Similarly, Saint Christopher was the patron saint of travelers, and Saint Cecilia offered special consideration to musicians who sought her help.

Some patron saints specialized not in a class of people, but in a particular geographic district. Saint Patrick, for example, has long been considered the patron saint of Ireland. Saint George serves a similar role for England, as does Saint Joan—also known as Joan of Arc—for France. Smaller areas, too, often sought out patron saints to bring their own interests to God's attention. "Every region or even every city or parish [should] venerate its own patron with particular honors,"[56] suggested one medieval author. Directing respect and prayers to a local patron, the people of the Middle Ages believed, would help earn God's favor for their whole community.

Shrines and Relics

If saints were unusually holy people, it followed that places associated with the lives of the saints were holy as well. Thus, Christians of the period were eager to visit shrines: graves, tombs, and other places important in the lives of the saints. Some of these shrines were believed to have miraculous powers, especially where healing was concerned.

Relics and Authenticity

From a modern vantage point, it is clear that relatively few medieval relics were genuine. While relics associated with recently dead and little-known saints may indeed have been authentic, others had nothing whatever to do with the saint in question. At best, they were objects that had come into contact with genuine relics somewhere along the way. These were called third-class relics, and they were thought to have a small amount of power to perform miracles. At worst, they were outright frauds passed off as genuine by enterprising con men. Faked relics were common enough that one such hoaxer, the Pardoner, appears in Geoffrey Chaucer's epic poem *Canterbury Tales*.

But the implications of fraud did not disturb Christian thinkers of the period. No one seemed to mind, for instance, that dozens of European churches claimed to own the actual nails used to fasten Jesus to the cross, even though legend insisted that there were no more than four, or that the various relics of Mary added up to a good deal more than one lower-class woman of her time and place could possibly have owned. Instead, Christians of the period continued to flock to see every relic they could find.

A sick person who visited such a shrine and directed a prayer to the saint associated with it, medieval Europeans agreed, could significantly improve his or her chances of being cured.

Shrines were sacred, but relics—objects and body parts associated with a saint—were valued even more highly. Part of the fascination with relics was the possibility that they might contain some element of the miraculous powers attributed to the saint. This notion dates to the earliest years of Christianity. "God worked extraordinary miracles at the hands of Paul," reads Acts 19:11–12. "When handkerchiefs or cloths which had touched his skin were applied to the sick, their diseases were cured and evil spirits departed from them." Even after many generations, some of these relics were believed to have unusual curative powers.

The use of relics was also thought to increase the odds that a prayer would reach God's ears. Aquinas likened relics to magnifying glasses that focused the light of God's grace on the person asking for help. Regardless of the specific ways in which relics worked, there was no question that they were prized by early and medieval Christians alike. The bones of Polycarp were described as "more valuable than precious gems, more costly than gold."[57] Virtually every Christian church of any size during the Middle Ages had at least a few relics, all of them used fervently in prayers of petition, and some in prayers of adoration as well.

Medieval relics came in many different forms. Some were said to be physical remains of the saint: for example, teeth, bones, hair clippings. Other relics included crosses, jewelry, or clothing that had belonged to the saint. In the case of martyrs, relics occasionally included items used in the saint's torture and killing. Most relics belonged to individual churches, which typically charged fees to those who wished to see or handle them. During a festive celebration in Rome in 1350, notes Barbara Tuchman, the church "raked in lavish offerings"[58] from those eager to view relics.

A Sense of Control

In truth, the point was not the relics' authenticity, but their purpose. Like

Holy Roman emperor Charles IV (right) receives the thorn relics from the crown of Jesus in this fourteenth-century fresco.

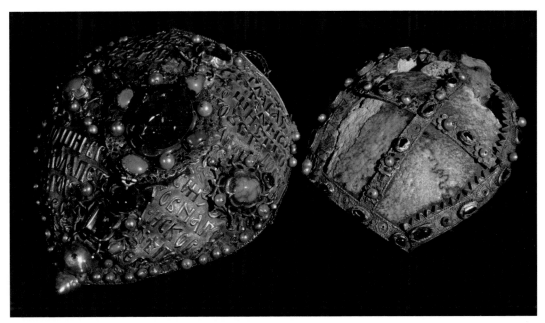

Pictured are relics purportedly of St. John the Baptist's skull. It was believed that relics possibly contained elements of a saint's powers.

prayer, like miracles, like saints in general, relics were important because they offered medieval Europeans a sense of control. The world of the Middle Ages was unpredictable and often frightening. It was a world populated by robbers and dragons, buffeted by storms and droughts, and beset by pestilence and injustice. Life in medieval Europe was harsh and often brutal, and it was easy for the people of the Middle Ages to conclude that humans had no control over it whatever.

Yet the medieval worldview did not completely accept that lack of control. As Europeans of the Middle Ages saw it, all events on earth were expressions of the conscious will of God. The people of the time tried to sway the will of God in their favor by speeding human requests to him. The notion that God could be influenced was an essential aspect of the medieval mind. Saints, miracles, relics, and prayer were all ways of exerting that influence and making life on earth a bit easier.

Chapter Six

SUPERSTITION AND MAGIC

Medieval Europeans relied in part on prayers of petition to help them gain a sense of control over their world. Of course, as the disastrous famines and horrendous years of plague showed, prayer did not always bring about the desired results. When that was the case, the people of the Middle Ages often reasoned that the fault must lie with themselves rather than with God. They responded by stepping up the intensity of their prayers or by trying to pray with greater sincerity. Sometimes this had an apparent effect; sometimes it did not.

But medieval Europeans did not rely solely on prayer to achieve an appearance of control over their fate. When prayer failed, and sometimes before it was even tried, the Europeans of the Middle Ages also used magic, superstition, and witchcraft to influence events in their favor. These measures drew on pagan customs and folk traditions that dated from the years before the arrival of Christianity in Europe. These pagan superstitions, then, also gave the medieval mind its distinctive character.

Folk Culture

The word "paganism" is a general and somewhat vague term most often used to describe religions that are polytheistic — that is, they acknowledge more than one god. Although modern historians know relatively little about the specific religious practices of Europeans prior to the advent of Christianity, it is clear that the religious thought of the time can be described as pagan. It is also clear that

Medieval patients undergo a folk treatment of cupping. Heated cups were applied to the skin to create a vacuum and pull pain and inflammation from deep in the body.

despite medieval Europe's overall allegiance to Christianity, many of the traditions and rituals of pagan Europe were still current long after Christianity became a dominant faith. Together, these traditions formed a widespread and influential folk culture that sometimes existed peacefully with Christianity—and sometimes battled with it for supremacy among the people of the Middle Ages.

One example of the power of this folk culture involved medieval medicine. Ignorant of how disease was spread and uncertain how to fight it, medieval doctors often had very little idea of how to treat a patient, especially when complaints involved internal organs that could not be seen without surgery. As a result, cures varied considerably and drew on many different theories and sources. Tuchman notes that the remedies offered by doctors of the time "ranged from the empiric [scientific] and sensible to the magical, with little distinction made between one and the other."[59]

Certainly the records of medieval society are filled with "magical" cures, used both by doctors—men formally trained in the most up-to-date theories of medicine—and by rural folk healers, many of them women, who relied on techniques from earlier eras. Medicines used to relieve symptoms during the Black Death, notes Tuchman, included everything from "pills of powdered stag's horn or myrrh and saffron to potions of potable gold."[60] Moreover, patients were often told to wear charms believed to have special healing powers

or asked to repeat magic chants, also known as incantations.

These remedies had obvious connections with earlier pagan ideas. In pre-Christian Europe, incantations were often directed toward gods who were thought to be responsible for healing. Charms, likewise, were believed to protect against evil spirits that caused disease. During the Middle Ages, though, cures often combined Christian ideas with folk remedies from much earlier times. To cure epilepsy, for instance, a doctor of the 1300s prescribed "the reading of the Gospel over the [patient] while simultaneously placing on him the hair of a white dog."[61]

Many Europeans of the Middle Ages were comfortable with the fact that healers and doctors drew cures from both folk medicine and Christian principles. When people were sick, they focused mainly on finding a remedy that worked, not on the origin of that remedy. Nor was there evidence that cures grounded in ancient superstitions were generally less effective than the more overtly Christian methods. On the contrary, the use of traditional cures, at least those involving herbs and roots, was often surprisingly successful. Careful observation by traditional healers over a period of many years had helped establish which plants were effective in the treatment of which diseases.

Witchcraft

Some folk treatments, however, aroused the anger of the established church—

Medieval women use candles and a goat in their practice of witchcraft, a philosophy that many Christians believed could be used to harm others.

and by extension, some of the ordinary Christians of the day. This was particularly true of remedies that seemed to call on evil spirits or those that appeared to rely on a suspension of the ordinary laws of nature. Many Christian officials feared that these magical techniques could be used to bring evil into the world. As historian Sharan Newman points out, "If magic can heal, then it stands to reason that it can also harm."[62]

Christian theologians concluded that those who used such magical treatments were sorcerers or witches—people who not only believed in the power of evil spirits, but actually worshipped the devil as well.

The issue of witchcraft was of great concern for the church during much of the Middle Ages. Throughout the medieval period, Christians believed absolutely in the existence of so-called

Witchcraft Trials

The records of most medieval witchcraft trials are lost to history. Those that remain offer fantastical descriptions of the lives supposedly led by witches. The following is taken from a contemporary synopsis of the 1477 trial of a French farm woman, Antoine Rose. In the narrative, Rose has recently met a mysterious man named Massetus Garini.

In the evening between 9 and 10 PM [Massetus] called for her and took her to . . . a synagogue [a gathering of witches] of many men and women enjoying themselves and *dancing backwards*. She was frightened and wished to withdraw, but Massetus persuaded her to do homage to the demon, in the shape of a dark man, called Robinet, who promised her plenty of gold and silver, speaking in a hoarse, almost unintelligible voice. Under his persuasion and that of others present she renounced God and the faith, kissed him on the foot, and promised him yearly tribute. . . . [Robinet] gave her a stick 18 inches long and a pot of ointment; she would anoint the stick with it, place it between her legs and say "Go; in the name of the devil, go!" and at once she would be transported through the air to the synagogue.

Quoted in Norman F. Cantor, *The Medieval Reader.* New York: HarperCollins, 1994, p. 257.

black magic. It was widely agreed that witches could use their powers to poison water supplies, kill children, and make crops sicken and die. Church leaders were swift to respond to charges that a person was doing harm through the use of pagan spells.

Though anxiety about witchcraft was present throughout the Middle Ages, fear of witches became especially pronounced toward the end of the period. During these years, the number of Europeans accused of witchcraft began to soar. The rising anxiety surrounding witchcraft, moreover, meant that a mere accusation usually sealed the fate of the supposed sorcerer. "Suspected witches were routinely put on trial," notes a modern author, writing of the late Middle Ages, "always with the presumption that they were guilty."[63]

Indeed, trials for witchcraft during the late medieval period were usually shams. Evidence against the accused was generally meager and indirect. Those suspected of sorcery—most of them women, many of them old—were tortured in an effort to get them to confess. Most eventually broke down under the brutal treatment and admitted to being witches. Even cooperation and repentance did not always save their lives, however. "You shall not allow a sorceress to live," reads the biblical book of Exodus 22:18, and medieval courts often applied the death penalty to those convicted of practicing magic.

Today, historians generally agree that the church's pursuit of witches was wrong and shameful, and that many, if not most, of those accused of sorcery had no intention of causing harm to anyone. Yet there is no question that many medical treatments used during the medieval period did indeed rely on elements of superstition and magic. Since these folk remedies did not appear to stem from God, church leaders believed themselves justified in trying to destroy them. The energy the church spent battling the problem of witchcraft indicates the power and prevalence of superstitious belief in the medieval way of thinking.

Astrology

Astrology, or the belief that the stars and planets control people's destinies, was another example of a folk or pagan tradition that remained popular during the medieval period. Most pagan societies made use of astrology to foretell the future and to try to make sense of their world. Messages in the movements of the planets and the positions of the stars could tell a farmer when to plant and a king when to launch an attack against an enemy. The trick was to learn to read the messages—and then to interpret their meaning correctly.

Astrology was widely accepted by the ancient Greeks and Romans, and the astrological ideas of these early civilizations carried over into Europe during the Middle Ages. However, astrology did not have the support of the medieval church. Though the Bible contains references to astrology—the Gospel of Matthew, for instance, mentions an unusually bright star that indicated Jesus's birth—the medieval church rejected the notion that the future could be foretold in the stars. Among other concerns, astrology seemed to place the stars above God in directing the affairs of the universe. "How is any room left for God to pass judgment on the deeds of men," demanded Augustine, writing in the 400s, "if they are subject to astrological forces?"[64]

Still, despite official condemnation, astrological thinking was widespread in medieval Europe. Comets and unusual astronomical events were commonly taken as signs of what was to come. Jean Froissart, for instance, took pains to note that a glorious and unexpected English military victory had been accompanied by a "very terrible eclipse of the sun."[65] After seeing a comet, a Dutch writer predicted a coming famine. Several Swedes who saw an unexpected reddish light in the night sky feared that it presaged an outbreak of disease.

As the Middle Ages continued, reliance on astrology increased. That was perhaps particularly true during the Black Death, when nothing seemed to halt or even slow the epidemic. A group of French doctors, for instance, developed a theory of the plague's outbreak that combined ideas from both astronomy and astrology. "On 20 March 1345, at 1:00 P.M.," they explained, "a conjunction of three higher planets—Saturn, Jupiter, and Mars—in the sign of Aquarius caused a corruption of the surrounding air."[66] Though inaccurate, the theory reflected the mood of a society desperate for answers—and desperate to exert some measure of control over its fate.

Despite the church's official position against astrology, medieval Christian leaders did not spend much time or energy challenging the practice. During the Middle Ages, there was no frenzy of

Pictured is a thirteenth-century zodiac chart. Astrology was widely accepted during the Middle Ages.

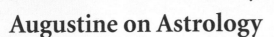

Augustine on Astrology

Saint Augustine had a number of reasons, theological and practical, to doubt the validity of astrology. In this excerpt from his book City of God, *Augustine details one of his greatest stumbling blocks where astrology is concerned: the problem of twins.*

How is it that [astrologers] have never been able to explain why there is such diversity in the life of twins: in their actions, their fortunes, their professions, their trades, their honors and in all the other things pertaining to human life and even in their death? It commonly happens that in these respects the twins resemble many strangers more than they resemble each other. And yet in birth they were separated by a very brief interval of time, and in conception they were begotten at one moment.

Interdisciplinary Documentation on Religion and Science. Quoted in "Augustine of Hippo: A Critique to Astrology from *The City of God.*" www.disf.org/en/documentation/01-Augustine2.asp.

activity against astrology as there had been against witchcraft. Those who tried to read the stars were not thrown into jail and put to death, as had happened to their counterparts suspected of sorcery. Although astrology had clearly sprung from pagan roots, church officials evidently believed that the practice was more of a distraction than a grave error. As a result, they let this manifestation of folk culture more or less alone.

Alchemy

The church held a similar attitude toward alchemy, a practice that held that any material could be transformed into any other. Like astrology, alchemy was accepted in most folk traditions. To a degree, alchemy was scientific and systematic; it is often considered today to be the forerunner of modern chemistry. By probing and testing, alchemists found dozens of ways to change the forms of various materials and developed several important theories about the nature of matter. In their research, medieval alchemists also discovered nitric acid, sulfuric acid, and a few other substances.

Like astrology, however, alchemy was not truly a science. Instead, it relied on a way of thinking that was, in the words of Friedrich Heer, "deeply entangled with magic and sorcery."[67] In part, the magic lay with the goals of alchemy, which often conflicted with the observed rules of nature. Alchemists believed, for example, that they could turn lead into gold, create a substance that would restore youth, or develop a medicine that could cure any disease. Alchemists also believed that success or failure in these pursuits depended on their own characteristics. Producing pure gold, alchemists agreed, required a pure spirit.

The magical roots of alchemy worried the church. Although church officials were at times intrigued by the scientific aspects of the practice, and even authorized Aquinas to study alchemy at one point, the discipline seemed too grounded in superstition to be truly acceptable. But as had been the case with astrology, the church did not use its resources to attack the practice. Instead, it simply encouraged its people not to engage in alchemy.

That disapproval, however, had very little effect. Tuchman calls alchemy "the most popular applied science"[68] of the period. Though relatively few people had the time and the means to undertake alchemy as a full-time pursuit, those who did threw themselves into the practice with great enthusiasm. Some alchemists devoted virtually their entire adult lives to the quest for gold and magical elixirs. Once again, the interest in alchemy reflected a desire of medieval Europeans to obtain a sense of control over their world—even if the methods they were using were not entirely acceptable in the eyes of the established Christian Church.

A Blending of Tradition

Prayer and incantations, saints and evil spirits, the power of God and the power of the planets—the medieval worldview thus included elements from two distinct traditions. Yet Christianity and paganism were more similar than they often appeared to be. The influences of the two systems in medicine were difficult to disentangle, of course, but there was more. The Christian notion of miracles— events that did not follow the laws of nature—bore a strong resemblance to the folk ideas of alchemy and astrology. And patron saints, as one writer puts it, took on "the same roles that the pagan gods . . . had fulfilled for centuries."[69]

The similarities between the two traditions were no coincidence. Many historians argue, in fact, that early Christians intentionally created traditions and rituals similar to those of the pagans. "The main concern of the [early] Church," writes Sharan Newman, "was the eradication of paganism. One way this was done was to provide an alternate to the pagan gods responsible for healing."[70] To accomplish this, Newman adds, Christians introduced the concept of intercessor saints, who filled much the same role as the original pagan deities. The similarities between pagan gods and Christian saints, in Newman's view, encouraged the growth of Christianity in the region.

Holidays are another example. Before the arrival of Christianity, the Romans celebrated the rebirth of the sun god Mithras at the time of the winter solstice each December. When Christianity began to grow in influence, it developed a festival of its own that incorporated some elements of the Mithras celebration— including, most notably, the time of year.

This festival, of course, was Christmas, which honored the birth of Jesus.

At the time and afterward, some church leaders flatly rejected the idea that the birth celebrations of Jesus and Mithras had anything to do with one another. Jesus, they pointed out, was the Son of God; Mithras was just another deity in a culture that worshipped many. "We hold this day holy," wrote a

An alchemist and his assistants conduct an experiment in this illustration from a fifteenth-century manuscript.

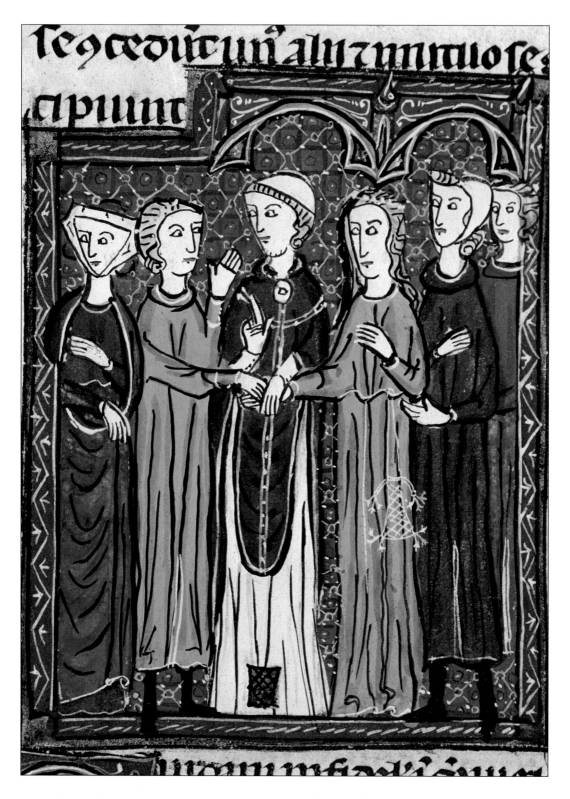

86 Miracles, Saints, and Superstition: The Medieval Mind

A thirteenth-century manuscript depicts a priest blessing a marriage. Medieval priests blessed weddings, burials, and even food.

theologian in the 300s, "not like the pagans because of the birth of the sun, but because of him who made it."[71] Many modern historians, though, believe that Christmas was instituted specifically to allow an easier transition to Christianity for Romans already accustomed to a solstice festival.

Pagan and Christian

During the Middle Ages, indeed, the lives of most Europeans reflected this mix of pagan culture and Christian ideas. Priests blessed marriages and buried the dead according to Christian ritual, but as Jeffrey Singman notes, clergy were also asked "to provide blessings for salt, butter, and cheese, to bless eggs at Easter and seeds at planting time."[72] Healers tried remedies for disease that stemmed from pagan customs as well as from Christian ways of thinking. During times of crisis, some Europeans prayed to patron saints, some wore charms to keep away the evil spirits, and many did both. Pagan superstition was not eliminated by the onset of Christianity in Europe. Instead, in ways large and small, obvious and obscure, it was incorporated into the rites and rituals of the established church.

That blend of ideas made sense for the people of the Middle Ages, too. The outlook for medieval Europeans was often bleak. Life was unpredictable; the world was unforgiving; dangers lurked everywhere. Under these conditions, it was reasonable for the people of medieval Europe to reach for every shred of comfort and control they could find. That meant saints and magic spells, astrology along with miracles, Christian ritual leavened by ancient folk beliefs. The medieval world was large enough and complex enough to incorporate both —and in the long run, it was frightening enough to require both as well.

A CHANGING WORLDVIEW

Medieval society was never completely stagnant, but in the 1400s the pace of change began to accelerate. In the space of a few decades, the world of the Middle Ages disappeared and was replaced by a period known as the Renaissance, or "rebirth," which was marked by great interest in art, commerce, and learning. The Renaissance began in Italy, the home of artists and thinkers such as Leonardo da Vinci, Michelangelo, and Galileo, and soon spread through the rest of Europe. As the ideas of the Renaissance swept across Europe, they caused great changes in European society.

These changes were significant. During the 1400s the old system of feudalism, already in decline, collapsed entirely in favor of a growing sense of national identity and unity. Explorers sailed around Africa, ventured to eastern Asia, and crossed the Atlantic Ocean to the Americas. Johannes Gutenberg developed movable type, making it possible to mass produce books. Trade became increasingly vital, both within Europe and between Europeans and the outside world. There were new ideas in science, in technology, in government. Even the powerful Christian Church could not entirely withstand the changes in the air. In 1517 a young monk named Martin Luther sparked the Protestant Reformation, which eventually split the church in two.

The Renaissance, then, was dramatically different in many ways from the Middle Ages. The changes that took place during this period were fundamentally the product of a new worldview, a mindset in some ways the opposite of the one that had prevailed during medieval times. The medieval period was an inward-looking time marked by fear of what lay beyond Europe's borders, for example, whereas the Renaissance was an outward-looking era marked by deep curiosity about the greater world. It was therefore no coincidence that serious exploration of the outside world did not begin until the Renaissance was under way. Gutenberg's printing press, similarly, was a triumph of ingenuity—but a triumph made possible by a society in which experimentation was valued in a way it had not been during the Middle Ages.

In effect, the Middle Ages came to a close in part because a new worldview permitted and encouraged changes in society. During the Middle Ages, for instance, no great astronomical discovery called into question the notion of an earth-centered universe. But the fresh spirit of inquiry that marked the Renaissance allowed men such as Copernicus and Galileo to defy conventional wisdom by demonstrating that in fact the earth orbited the sun, not the other way around. Similarly, no medieval heresy succeeded in fracturing the church, but Luther caused an irreparable split soon after prevailing attitudes

Martin Luther (right, holding up two fingers) participates in a fevered discussion about religion. In 1517, he started the Protestant Reformation, which divided the church into two sects.

Galileo shows his telescope to the doge of Venice. The Middle Ages came to a close when new scientific, political, and religious theories were encouraged.

and assumptions began to shift. And the changes in science, commerce, politics, and art during the Renaissance reflected a new way of thinking, a mindset that valued and accepted change in a way that was not generally true for medieval Europeans.

The medieval passion for order, emphasis on religion, and devotion to saints and miracles guided the people of the Middle Ages through many difficult years. In many ways, this worldview worked. It offered medieval Europeans a sense of comfort, a vestige of control, and a way of organizing a complex and often intimidating world. In some sense, though, Europe could not have developed further until there was a change in its mindset—an emphasis on discovery, a rise in curiosity, and a higher value on creativity. More than the specific changes in science, commerce, and art that accompanied the Renaissance, it was the arrival of a new worldview that marked the close of the medieval period in Europe.

Notes

Chapter 1: Christianity and the Medieval Mind

1. Norman F. Cantor, ed., *The Encyclopedia of the Middle Ages.* New York: Viking, 1999, p. 120.
2. Charles Panati, *Sacred Origins of Profound Things.* New York: Penguin, 1996, p. 373.
3. Barbara Tuchman, *A Distant Mirror: The Calamitous 14th Century.* New York: Knopf, 1978, p. 34.
4. Quoted in Norman F. Cantor, *The Medieval Reader.* New York: HarperCollins, 1994, p. 354.
5. Quoted in Tuchman, *Distant Mirror*, p. 34.
6. Eileen Power, *Medieval People.* London: Methuen, 1963, p. 81.
7. Cantor, *Encyclopedia of the Middle Ages*, p. 121.
8. Quoted in Cantor, *Medieval Reader*, p. 50.
9. Quoted in Friedrich Heer, *The Medieval World.* New York: New American Library, 1961, p. 55.
10. Quoted in Cantor, *Medieval Reader*, p. 54.
11. Cantor, *Encyclopedia of the Middle Ages*, p. 336.
12. Jeffrey L. Singman, *Daily Life in Medieval Europe.* Westport, CT: Greenwood, 1999, p. 12.

Chapter 2: Time and Space

13. Cantor, *Encyclopedia of the Middle Ages*, p. 126.
14. Quoted in Cantor, *Medieval Reader*, p. 81.
15. Quoted in Walter Ullman, *The Origins of the Great Schism: A Study in Fourteenth-Century Ecclesiastical History.* North Haven, CT: Archon, 1967, p. 21.
16. Quoted in Jennifer Ward, *Women of the English Nobility and Gentry, 1066–1500.* New York: Manchester University Press, 1995, p. 118.
17. Adam Usk, *The Chronicle of Adam Usk*, ed. and trans. C. Given-Wilson. Oxford: Clarendon, 1997, p. 59.
18. Quoted in Cantor, *Medieval Reader*, p. 285.
19. Jeffrey Burton Russell, *A History of Medieval Christianity: Prophecy and Order*, New York: Crowell, 1968, p. 85.
20. Quoted in Cantor, *Medieval Reader*, p. 96.
21. Cantor, *Encyclopedia of the Middle Ages*, p. 414.
22. Heer, *Medieval World*, p. 38.
23. Quoted in Robin Hallett, *The Penetration of Africa: European Exploration in North and West Africa*

to 1815. New York: Praeger, 1965, p. 49.

Chapter 3: An Ordered Universe

24. Alexander Jones, ed., *The Jerusalem Bible*. Garden City, NY: Doubleday, 1966, p. 49.
25. Russell, *History of Medieval Christianity*, p. 83.
26. Cantor, *Encyclopedia of the Middle Ages*, pp. 51–52.
27. Charles Freeman, *The Closing of the Western Mind: The Rise of Faith and the Fall of Reason*. New York: Knopf, 2003, p. 319.
28. Freeman, *Closing of the Western Mind*, p. 319.
29. Russell, *History of Medieval Christianity*, pp. 53–54.
30. Panati, *Sacred Origins of Profound Things*, p. 63.
31. Panati, *Sacred Origins of Profound Things*, p. 70.

Chapter 4: A Disorderly World

32. Quoted in Tuchman, *Distant Mirror*, p. 98.
33. Quoted in Cantor, *Medieval Reader*, p. 281.
34. Quoted in Cantor, *Medieval Reader*, p. 277.
35. Quoted in Tuchman, *Distant Mirror*, p. 41.
36. Russell, *History of Medieval Christianity*, p. 57.
37. Quoted in Freeman, *Closing of the Western Mind*, p. 316.
38. Quoted in William Chester Jordan, *The Great Famine: Northern Europe in the Early Fourteenth Century*. Princeton, NJ: Princeton University Press, 1996, p. 22.
39. Quoted in Tuchman, *Distant Mirror*, p. 109.
40. Cantor, *Medieval Reader*, p. 29.
41. Quoted in Singman, *Daily Life in Medieval Europe*, p. 74.
42. Russell, *History of Medieval Christianity*, p. 86.

Chapter 5: Miracles, Prayers, and Relics

43. Quoted in Jacques Le Goff, ed., *The Medieval World*. London: Parkgate, 1997, p. 150.
44. Panati, *Sacred Origins of Profound Things*, p. 4.
45. Quoted in Jordan, *Great Famine*, p. 18.
46. Cantor, *Encyclopedia of the Middle Ages*, p. 162.
47. Quoted in Tuchman, *Distant Mirror*, p. 113.
48. Panati, *Sacred Origins of Profound Things*, p. 16.
49. Quoted in Donald Attwater, *The Penguin Dictionary of Saints*. New York: Viking Penguin, 1983, p. 281.
50. Quoted in Panati, *Sacred Origins of Profound Things*, p. 499.
51. Attwater, *Penguin Dictionary of Saints*, p. 12.

52. Panati, *Sacred Origins of Profound Things*, p. 510.
53. Russell, *History of Medieval Christianity*, p. 137.
54. Quoted in Tuchman, *Distant Mirror*, p. 33.
55. Paul B. Newman, *Daily Life in the Middle Ages*. Jefferson, NC: McFarland, 2001, pp. 263–64.
56. Quoted in Le Goff, *Medieval World*, p. 339.
57. Quoted in Panati, *Sacred Origins of Profound Things*, p. 254.
58. Tuchman, *Distant Mirror*, p. 127.

Chapter 6: Superstition and Magic

59. Tuchman, *Distant Mirror*, p. 110.
60. Tuchman, *Distant Mirror*, p. 111.
61. Quoted in Freeman, *Closing of the Western Mind*, p. 321.
62. Sharan Newman, *The Real History Behind the Da Vinci Code*. New York: Berkley, 2005, p. 320.
63. Cantor, *Encyclopedia of the Middle Ages*, p. 445.
64. Interdisciplinary Documentation on Religion and Science, "Augustine of Hippo: A Critique to Astrology from *The City of God*." www.disf.org/en/documentation/01-Augustine2.asp.
65. Quoted in Cantor, *Medieval Reader*, p. 26.
66. Quoted in Robert S. Gottfried, *The Black Death: Natural and Human Disaster in Medieval Europe*. New York: Free Press, 1983, p. 178.
67. Heer, *Medieval World*, p. 301.
68. Tuchman, *Distant Mirror*, p. 56.
69. Freeman, *Closing of the Western Mind*, p. 264.
70. Newman, *Real History Behind the Da Vinci Code*, p. 321.
71. Quoted in Panati, *Sacred Origins of Profound Things*, p. 216.
72. Singman, *Daily Life in Medieval Europe*, p. 13.

For Further Reading

Books

James Barter, *The Late Middle Ages*. San Diego: Lucent Books, 2006. A companion volume to Corrick's book listed below. Discusses war, government, religion, and other important aspects of the second half of the medieval era.

Norman F. Cantor, *The Medieval Reader*. New York: HarperCollins, 1994. Offers a variety of writings from the medieval period, grouped by subject, together with commentary. Includes examples of fiction as well as nonfiction.

Norman F. Cantor, ed., *The Encyclopedia of the Middle Ages*. New York: Viking, 1999. An excellent resource on the medieval period, with entries on people, places, and ideas. Well illustrated with color prints as well.

James A. Corrick, *The Early Middle Ages*. San Diego: Lucent Books, 2006. A thorough description of the world of the early medieval period. Includes information on the political and economic structures of the time as well as on the medieval church and the general way of thinking common to the period.

Editors of Time-Life Books, *What Life Was Like in the Age of Chivalry*. Alexandria, VA: Time-Life Books, 1997. Informative and beautifully illustrated. Describes many aspects of medieval life and customs, including some pertaining to the medieval way of thinking.

Edward D. English, *Encyclopedia of the Medieval World*. New York: Facts On File, 2004. A detailed sourcebook on many aspects of the Middle Ages.

Sylvia A. Johnson, *Mapping the World*. New York: Atheneum, 1999. A well-illustrated and informative book on the history of maps and mapmaking, with some detail on the maps of medieval times.

Carl Lindahl, John McNamara, and John Lindow, *Medieval Folklore: A Guide to Myths, Legendary Tales, and Customs*. New York: Oxford University Press, 2002. A large and thorough book, written for sophisticated readers, with plenty of information about medieval thought.

Tony McAleavy, *Life in a Medieval Abbey*. New York: Enchanted Lion, 2003. Well illustrated, with interesting information about medieval religious life and the Middle Ages in general.

Tony McAleavy, *Life in a Medieval Castle*. New York: Enchanted Lion, 2003. This informative book focuses on the way royalty and ordinary people lived during the Middle Ages.

Martha Newbigging, *Archers, Alchemists, and 98 Other Medieval Jobs You Might Have Loved or Loathed*. Toronto: Annick Press, 2003. A breezy book describing various aspects of medieval life and culture.

Paul B. Newman, *Daily Life in the Middle Ages*. Jefferson, NC: McFarland, 2001. Describes the characteristics of the medieval period. Includes short but useful sections on saints, magic, and superstition.

Charles Panati, *Sacred Origins of Profound Things*. New York: Penguin Arcana, 1996. Describes how many religious traditions got their start, including ideas that have to do with Christianity, Judaism, Islam, and other faiths. This book contains a wealth of information on saints, miracles, and the structure and theology of the medieval church. It is a fascinating work.

Jeffrey L. Singman, *Daily Life in Medieval Europe*. Westport, CT: Greenwood, 1999. A straightforward description of life in the Middle Ages, with information on monastic life, the lives of nobles, the lives of peasants, and more.

Includes some information on the medieval worldview.

Barbara Tuchman, *A Distant Mirror: The Calamitous 14th Century*. New York: Alfred A. Knopf, 1978. A long but intriguing—and generally readable—discussion of the 1300s and the calamities that took place during that century. Includes plenty of information about the Black Death, the wars of the period, and other aspects of medieval life and thought.

Web Resources

"Church and State," BBC History, www.bbc.co.uk/history/state/. An informative site dealing specifically with the history of Christianity in Great Britain, but more generally with the issues of churches and governments as well. Includes documents, essays, and background information on the medieval church and related topics.

"Index of Cartographic Images Illustrating Maps of the Early Medieval Period," www.henry-davis.com/MAPS /EMwebpages/EML.html. Reproductions of maps of the Middle Ages.

"Internet Medieval Sourcebook," www.fordham.edu/halsall/sbook.html. An enormous archive of documents and other material relating to the medieval period; includes links to further information.

"Medieval History," www.timeref.org/. This site presents a time line of events throughout much of the medieval period, with a particular focus on the history of Britain.

"The ORB: On-line Reference Book for Medieval Studies," www.the-orb.net/encyclo.html. An online encyclopedia with articles and links that deal with the Middle Ages.

Index

Michelangelo, 88
middle class, 58
Milton, John, 48
miracles, 68
Miracles of the Virgin, 70
Mithras (Roman sun god), 84, 85
monks, 21
Muslims, 17

Newman, 84
Newman, Paul B., 72
Newman, Sharan, 79
Nibelungenlied, 64
nobles, 58
nuns, 21

Odo (archbishop of Rouen), 21
order, medieval philosophy and, 49, 57–58

paganism, 76
    similarities between Christianity and, 84–85, 87
Panati, Charles, 18, 48
Patrick (saint), 72
Paul (apostle), 64, 73
peasants, 58
Petrarch, 20–21
Philip (saint), 68
philosophy, medieval, focus on order in, 49, 57–58
pilgrimages, 31
Pliny the Elder, 36
Polo, Marco, 31
Polycarp (bishop), 68, 73
pope, power of, 21–22
prayer, 62

forms of, 64–65
    of petition, 65
Protestant Reformation, 20, 88
Ptolemy, 40–41
purgatory, 18–19

relics, 72–73
    purpose of, 74–75
Renaissance, change in worldview and coming of, 89–90
Roman Catholic Church
    astrology and, 81–83
    hierarchy of, 21–22, 57
    money and, 20
    the state and, 23–24
    witchcraft and, 79–80, 81
Roman Empire, Christianity and, 16–17
Rose, Antoine, 80
Roussiaud, Jacques, 62
Russell, Jeffrey Burton, 30, 40, 55

saints, 68, 70
    patron, 70, 72, 84
Satan, 18, 48
    Albigensian heresy on, 24
Saxons, 16
seasons, as basic unit of time, 30, 37
serfs, 58
shrines, 72–73
Singman, Jeffrey, 24, 87
society
    feudal, hierarchy of, 58, 60
    medieval
        change in worldview of, 89–90
        insularity of, 33, 35
Southern, R.W., 70

Picture Credits

Cover image: © Elio Ciol/CORBIS
akg-images, 85
Alamy Images, 11
Art Resource, NY, 31
Biblioteca Monasterio del Escorial, Madrid, Spain/Giraudon/Bridgeman
    Art Library, 82
Bibliotheque Municipale, Laon, France/Bridgeman Art Library, 86
Bibliotheque Nationale, Paris, France/ Giraudon/Bridgeman Art Library, 71
Bildarchiv Preussischer Kulturbesitz/Art Resource, NY, 15, 56, 89
British Library, London, UK/Bridgeman Art Library, 34
Cameraphoto/Art Resource, NY, 47
Erich Lessing/Art Resource, NY, 19, 35, 41
Giraudon/Art Resource, NY, 59
HIP/Art Resource, NY, 42
Karlstejn Castle, Czech Republic/ Giraudon/Bridgeman Art Library, 74
Maury Aaseng, 32
Musee des Beaux-Arts, Tournai, Belgium/Bridgeman Art Library, 51
Musee Marmottan, Paris, France/ Giraudon/Bridgeman Art Library, 55
National Trust/Art Resource, NY, 63
Palazzo Pubblico, Siena, Italy/ Alinari/Bridgeman Art Library, 26
Reunion des Musees Nationaux/ Art Resource, NY, 29
Scala/Art Resource, NY, 12, 53, 90
The Art Archive/Bibliotheque Mazarine Paris/Dagli Orti, 66
The Art Archive/Bibliotheque Municipale Moulins/Dagli Orti, 45
The Art Archive/Bodleian Library Oxford, 79
The Art Archive/Dagli Orti, 69
The Art Archive/Museo Civico Cristiano Brescia/Dagli Orti, 16
The Art Archive/Oldsaksammlung Oslo/Dagli Orti, 39
The Art Archive/San Nicola Basilica Tolentino/Dagli Orti, 22
The Art Archive/University Library Prague/Dagli Orti, 77
Werner Forman/Art Resource, NY, 75

About the Author

Stephen Currie is the author of more than forty books, including a number of works on history and some historical fiction. Among his books for Lucent are *Life in a Wild West Show*, *The Olympic Games*, and *Adoption*. He is also a teacher. He grew up in Illinois and now lives with his family in upstate New York.

WITHDRAWN